Alcohol Related Problems

Linda Hunt

HEINEMANN EDUCATIONAL BOOKS
LONDON

Heinemann Educational Books Ltd
22 Bedford Square, London WC1B 3HH
LONDON EDINBURGH MELBOURNE AUCKLAND
HONG KONG SINGAPORE KUALA LUMPUR NEW DELHI
IBADAN NAIROBI JOHANNESBURG
EXETER (NH) KINGSTON PORT OF SPAIN

First published 1982

British Library Cataloguing in Publication Data

Hunt, Linda
Alcohol related problems. –
(Community care practice handbooks; 7)
1. Alcoholism – Social aspects
I. Title II. Series
362.2'923 HV5035

ISBN 0-435-82450 3

Phototypesetting by Georgia Origination, Liverpool
Printed in Great Britain by Biddles Ltd., Guildford, Surrey

Contents

Acknowledgements

The opportunities afforded me to work with many challenging, resourceful and courageous people with alcohol related problems made it possible for me to consider writing this book and I owe these unnamed people a debt of gratitude.

I have received invaluable help from many friends and colleagues who have discussed ideas with me and read draft chapters. I am particularly grateful for helpful comments contributed by Alan Cartwright, Senior Psychotherapist, Mount Zeehan Unit; David Colvin, Chief Social Work Adviser, Scottish Office; Pauline Hammond, Senior Social Work Adviser, Scottish Office; Mona McDonald, Extra Mural Department, University of Edinburgh; Ray Pavey, Senior Social Worker, Dingleton Hospital; Bruce Ritson, Consultant Psychiatrist, Royal Edinburgh Hospital; and Bryan Williams, Lecturer in Social Work, University of Dundee. Special thanks are due to Ray Drennan who typed and patiently retyped the manuscript.

The responsibility for the contents of the book is, of course, mine. The views expressed do not necessarily reflect Scottish Office policy.

1 A Drinking Society

The clay still clings to me here, and the heavy smell
Of peat and dung and cattle, and the taste of the dram
In my mouth, the last of all.
These things are what I was made for.

from *There's nothing here* by Edwin Muir

Britain is a society in which alcoholic beverages are readily available in high street supermarkets and off-licences, in which public houses are regarded as convenient places to meet with friends, and where it is unusual for an adult to be totally abstinent. The proportion of the population that abstains has declined steadily since the second world war, and it is estimated that not more than five men and 12 women in 100 are now totally abstinent (Dight 1976). There are places (in Scotland and Northern Ireland) and groups (e.g. Plymouth Brethren) in which abstinence is highly regarded, but it is no longer generally valued. It is now the norm for adults to drink – and on certain occasions it may be thought to be normal to become drunk. For most people drinking, and perhaps occasional drunkenness, is associated with pleasurable social activity. Most of us enjoy visiting a public house, with friends before the match on Saturday, or with colleagues at lunch time; and most of us enthusiastically participate in occasional parties and celebrations. Increasingly we also enjoy a bottle of wine with the main meal of the day.

Children and young people are interested in alcohol too, and research has revealed that they know a good deal about it (Jahoda and Crammond 1972; Davies and Stacey 1972; Aitken 1978). A study of children in Glasgow showed that by the age of six years two-fifths of children were able to distinguish some of the characteristics of alcohol. For example, some could distinguish types of bottle which usually contain alcoholic drinks, others recognised alcoholic drinks by their smell and identified typically drunken behaviour. Davies (1980) has drawn the conclusion that by the age of eight years 'a large majority of children have attained the concept of alcohol'. More than 80 per cent of primary school children have tasted an alcoholic drink, and by the time they are 14 years, 92 per cent of boys and 85 per cent of girls have tasted alcohol. The first experience of drinking is usually in their own homes and with their parents' consent. Hawker (1978) suggests that a third of boys and a quarter of girls aged 13–16 in England have a drink once a week or more often. Amongst her sample of 7,000, 16 per cent of boys and 10 per cent of girls reported they had been drunk on more than one occasion in the previous year. 98 per cent of boys and 96 per cent of girls have tasted an alcoholic drink by the time they are 17 years. Some have established a regular pattern of drinking by that age and many are drinking outside their own homes. As Stacey and Davies (1970) point out, 'Since drinking is an integral part of the life style of the clear majority of adults, the drinking behaviour of youth in general may be viewed as part of an anticipatory socialisation process and one of the normal concomitants of the transition from childhood to adulthood'.

During the last 20 years, as the real price of alcohol (in relation to other items of consumer spending) has decreased and disposal income has increased, the total amount of alcoholic drink consumed in Britain has steadily risen. The available statistics make it clear this increase is not simply a consequence of more people drinking: there has also been a significant rise in per capita consumption. The increase in the consumption of wine and spirits is especially marked. In 1960, 15 million gallons of spirits were consumed in the UK; by 1979 consumption had risen to 40 million gallons. Similarly, wine consumption in 1960 was 28 million gallons, but had risen to 100 million by 1979. Beer consumption has increased, but at a slower rate (27 million bulk barrels in 1960 to 41 million in 1979).

By 1978 alcohol accounted for about 8 per cent of total consumer spending, compared with 7 per cent in 1970 and 6.1 per cent in 1963. Over a period of approximately 10 years (1967–78) when consumer spending increased by 22.1 per cent, spending on alcohol increased by 66.4 per cent. Hawker (1979), noting that the Brewers' Society had announced that British beer drinkers consumed 11.5 billion pints in 1977, commented that 'taking the population as a whole that is the equivalent of 208 pints per person in that year'. Beverage alcohol is clearly a regular and important feature of the household budget.

During the last 20 years as public houses have become more attractive and the availability of alcoholic beverages through off-licences has increased (by 1977, 40 per cent of supermarkets were licensed to sell alcohol), the number of women who drink has steadily risen. It is often suggested that whilst drinking is now acceptable for women, intoxication is not and that excessive drinking in women tends to remain hidden because of the shame attached to it (Birchmore and Walderman 1975). Nevertheless, there has been a sharp increase in women referred to various helping agencies because of alcohol problems. For example, in 1956, 16.7 per cent of the people diagnosed alcoholic were women, but in 1977 the proportion of women had risen to 24.7 per cent and in 1978 more than a third of clients of one alcohol counselling service were women. There seem to be some differences between men and women in their typical drinking patterns before referral for help (e.g. women seem to start drinking at a slightly later age and to have a shorter history of excessive drinking before the onset of social and physical alcohol related problems) but there is no evidence to suggest women are less likely to respond to the offer of help than men. The ready availability of alcoholic beverages, the increased earning power of women and other changes in their position in our society may all have contributed to the increase in drinking and the rise in drinking problems amongst women (Shaw 1980), but women provide an example of a general trend that has recently become a matter of concern.

Evidence supporting the view that as alcohol consumption rises so does the proportion of the population suffering physical and/or social damage from excessive drinking has become increasingly convincing. The idea that a higher level of consumption is associated with a higher incidence of excessive drinking and alcohol dependence has been articulated in a variety of forms for two centuries or more. At different times it has been used in Britain and the USA as an argument for raising the tax on alcohol, for limiting or prohibiting its sale and for making a personal commitment to lifelong abstinence. Recently it has become possible to support the idea through the demonstration of a significant statistical relationship between the rate of consumption of alcohol and the incidence of alcohol related problems. Although it is *not* possible to describe the relationship in mathematical terms, it is possible to show that the most obvious indicators of alcohol abuse (i.e. death from cirrhosis of the liver; drunkenness offences) are closely associated with the level of consumption in a community (see Table 1).

The Semple and Yarrow (1974) graph (see Figure 1) of the relationship between the price of whisky, the level of consumption and hospital admissions for alcoholism dramatically reinforces the point.

The relationships illustrated here are not, of course, simply cause and effect. Other factors, such as the social acceptability of regular heavy drinking and the availability of alternative means of temporarily relieving stress (e.g. tranquillising drugs) will affect the

Table 1 Relationship between per capita consumption and key indicators of alcoholism

	1961	*1963*	*1965*	*1967*	*1969*	*1971*	*1973*	*1975*	*1977*
Per capita UK consumption (population of 15 years and over litres of absolute alcohol)*	6.2	6.2	6.5	6.7	7.0	7.7	7.9	8.9	9.8
UK deaths from cirrhosis	1,648	1,619	1,654	1,632	1,878	1,836	2,133	2,208	2,220
Drunkenness offences (England and Wales thousands)	74.7	83.0	73.0	75.5	80.5	86.7	99.3	103.2	103.3

* from Orford and Edwards 1978

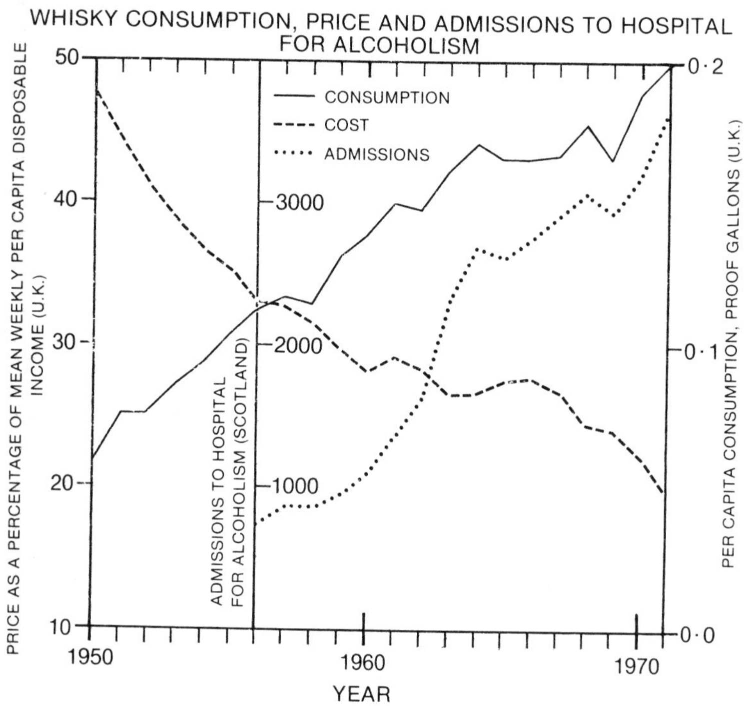

Figure 1 (from Semple and Yarrow 1974, Health Bulletin vol. 32 no. 1, Scottish Home and Health Department)

level of consumption. It seems clear, however, that when per capita consumption is reduced problems associated with alcohol abuse become less common. The chart reproduced in Figure 2 shows that convictions for drunkenness dropped dramatically when the permitted hours of opening of public houses were limited by statute during the first world war, and data from the USA show a decline in deaths from cirrhosis during the period of prohibition.

In 1967 when the Road Safety Act came into force, the public was made aware that it is dangerous to drink and drive. The association between drinking and road traffic accidents is very clear, with approximately one in five (i.e. 1,200 per annum) deaths caused by drivers having a blood alcohol level above the prescribed limit (Department of Transport 1980). Recently national newspapers have presented reports suggesting that accidental

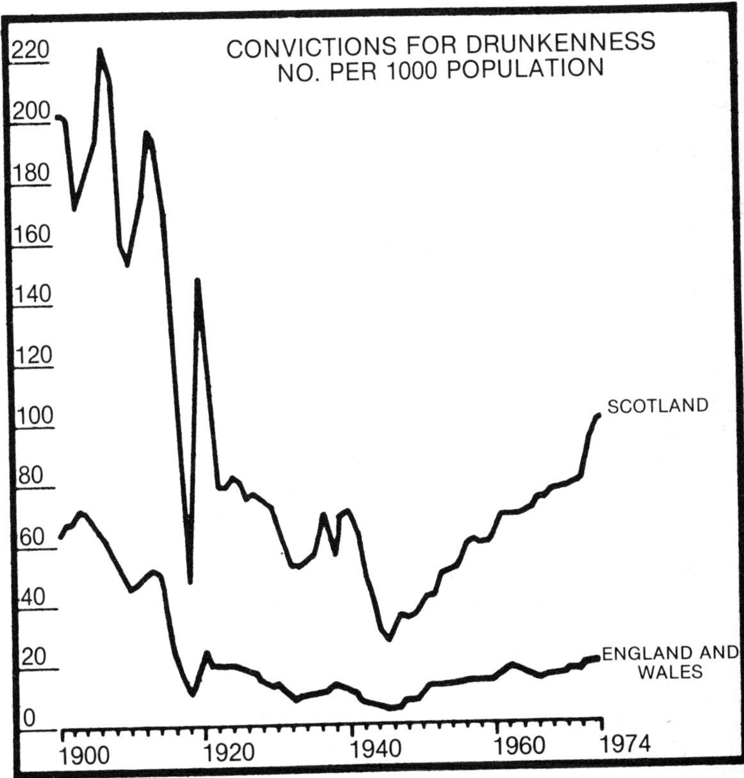

Figure 2 Copyright © New Society, London. Reprinted by permission.

deaths due to drowning and fire in the home are frequently associated with having a high level of alcohol in the bloodstream. Thus, over the last 20 years, as 'taking a drink' has become a regular and enjoyable activity for most men and women, information about the harm misuse of alcohol causes has become more freely available. During the same period the number and range of services specialising in helping those harmed through alcohol misuse to modify their drinking behaviour has increased, and their methods of work and the means of preventing alcohol problems have become the subjects of major research studies.

In the early 1960s these developments were accompanied by emphasis on a disease concept of alcoholism. More recently the notion that alcohol dependence is an illness appropriately treated in hospital has been challenged. It is now commonly regarded as a largely social problem with serious medical consequences. This shift in orientation has precipitated a change in the help offered to people experiencing difficulty in controlling their drinking.

Facilities for people with alcohol related problems

Twenty years ago the majority of people with alcohol problems receiving any service did so either through admission to a psychiatric unit or through Alcoholics Anonymous (AA). There was little interest in alcohol problems amongst the staff of psychiatric hospitals, and generally those diagnosed alcoholic and admitted to the hospitals were not felt to be helped by their experience. However, by 1962 the Ministry of Health, influenced by the work of Dr Glatt at Warlingham Park Hospital, was suggesting the development of regional hospital based units specialising in the treatment of alcoholics by group therapy. The emphasis in the Ministry's memorandum was on in-patient care, although the usefulness of out-patient follow-up and links with AA were mentioned (Ministry of Health 1962). At that time a book attempting to demonstrate that alcoholism is a disease which can be analysed and classified like any other, was having its impact (Jellinek 1960). The book was probably a highly significant influence in shifting helping agents such as doctors and social workers from a prejudiced and inappropriately moralistic interpretation of alcohol problems. It encouraged a perception of alcoholism that was similar to that of other 'relapsing illnesses' such as bronchitis, and consequently raised the expectation that it could be relieved by 'treatment' (Kessel and Walton 1965). A positive and hopeful view began to develop and was reinforced by the apparent success of Glatt's unit. By 1968 specialist alcoholism treatment units (ATUs) had been opened by 13 regional Hospital Boards and in 1977 there were 36 hospital treatment units in the UK, containing 619 beds. However, by 1977 a number of developments had occurred which challenged the position of ATUs as the primary source of expert help for all who have alcohol problems, and precipitated changes in the methods of intervention used in the units.

At the beginning of the 1970s the following facts were apparent:

1. people in social classes IV and V of the Registrar General's classification were under-represented amongst the patients of ATUs;
2. many people were not reaching helping agencies and continued to have severe problems;
3. some of those diagnosed alcoholic need help over a very long period of time (i.e. more than 12 months);
4. some people receive all the help they need whilst remaining out-patients of a treatment unit;
5. some people recover through the help of non-medical agencies such as AA;
6. some recover without contact with any helping agency.

As these facts became apparent, new services emerged and older ones changed. Attention was given to the needs of the homeless alcoholic; small hostel units were established for those who need longer term support after leaving ATUs; volunteer counselling services were introduced by local councils on alcoholism; day care facilities were developed and hospital units began to give more emphasis to out-patient work and to forging links with hostels and counsellors in their locality. The 1973 DHSS circular 'Community Services for Alcoholics' encouraged voluntary agencies to establish hostels and sometimes hostel care was offered as an alternative to hospital treatment. Later, detoxification centres established services designed for habitual drunken offenders.

During the 1970s, as the services changed and developed, research reports in Britain and America presented findings which challenged the appropriateness of the disease concept of alcoholism. The studies argued that whilst alcohol is a drug of dependence that causes and contributes to a wide range of physical illnesses, the existence of the illness 'alcoholism' is doubtful. Shaw *et al.* (1978) present an articulate summary of the process by which the disease concept came to be challenged and conclude that 'from a scientific viewpoint the disease theory of alcoholism has begun to seem less and less tenable. We are coming to realise that there are actually many factors involved in why a person comes to be harmed by his drinking' (p. 65). One consequence of this realisation is a shift from thinking about a single entity called alcoholism towards a concept of alcohol related harm (i.e. the constellation of medical, psychological and social problems which result from alcohol overuse). The shift (illustrated by one ATU being renamed 'alcohol problems clinic') has led to greater emphasis being given to the social and emotional problems that surround and flow from alcohol misuse.

The current position

Major changes are occurring in our understanding of alcohol abuse and the services likely to prove most helpful to the estimated 2–5 per cent of the population with alcohol related problems. One of the most important of these changes is the growing awareness that many people have the capacity to learn to control or abstain from drinking, and to achieve resolution of the problems consequent upon alcohol misuse, without admission to hospital units (inevitably expensive to run). The clinical and research evidence supporting this position is in turn leading to a new emphasis on primary care agents, such as general practitioners and social workers, as a major source of help for people with alcohol problems (Advisory Committee on Alcoholism 1978).

Two other factors emphasise the potential of social workers to be helpful. First, the scale of the social problems caused by alcohol misuse and the substantial numbers of clients of social workers in local authorities, probation and voluntary agencies who are harmed by alcohol, suggest that social workers are well placed to identify alcohol misuse and to initiate help designed to resolve the problems it has produced. Secondly, examination of the problems associated with the disease concept of alcoholism has encouraged the view that approaches to helping, like those used in social work practice, which aim to engage the active involvement of clients in the resolution of their problems seem likely to be the most helpful. It is now clear that one of the disadvantages for the individual of perceiving his* difficulties in medical terms is that once he has been defined and defines himself as 'ill' he may perceive the responsibility for making him 'well' as belonging to his doctor and the health services (Robinson 1976). This is a most unhelpful position to take, since a

* For the sake of brevity, where reference is made to the generality of clients or social workers the male pronoun is used throughout.

decision to modify drinking behaviour comes from and is sustained by the individual himself, not by the doctor or the health service. His willing co-operation is fundamental if any help offered is to be effective.

In summary, although our society is still characterised by confusion and ambivalence about its use of alcohol, research has helped to increase clarity about the social and medical problems alcohol can cause and practice has demonstrated that many people experiencing these problems can be helped to resume their normal functioning as competent and resourceful individuals.

2 Alcohol related problems

His eyes smear and his face grows fat
A dredged cadaver's except for tinge
Of diseased sunset through the sweat
Closing time strikes like a fatal attack
from *Report on Drinking Habits* by Vernon Scannell

Chapter 1 indicated that recent developments have prompted a reappraisal of perceptions of alcohol abuse. It introduced data which show that as per capita consumption of beverage alcohol rises, so does the proportion of the population harmed by excessive drinking, and suggested that whilst alcohol is properly described as a drug of dependence, it may not be appropriate to perceive alcoholism as a disease. These issues, and new questions raised by them, are currently the subject of careful study and vigorous debate and it is likely that a more detailed understanding of the nature of alcohol abuse and a further modification of definitions and terms will emerge in the future. In the mean time it is important to make the best use of what is already known.

Clarification of the known range of physical, psychological and social problems that result from alcohol abuse is a necessary preliminary to the examination of social work practice in situations in which misuse of alcohol is a concern. Clarity about the current use of terms such as 'alcoholism', 'dependence' and 'alcohol related problems' is necessary too.

Terms and context

The disease concept of alcoholism has been an important aid to the development of services for people with alcohol related problems. The World Health Organisation (1952) encouraged acceptance of a medical model of alcoholism, and this was substantially reinforced by Jellinek (1960). The perception of alcoholism then being promulgated discouraged the view that alcohol abuse was a sign of weakness or moral degeneracy, and at that time of optimism about health care in general and psychiatry in particular, encouraged the expectation that help (i.e. treatment) could be devised to cure the problem (i.e. disease). However, research and practice during the last 20 years have shown that 'alcoholism' is not a single disease entity which can be described through the listing of specific signs and symptoms which appear in a predictable order. This has emerged through the demonstration of a number of important facts.

1. The types of alcohol problems experienced will be influenced by:
   (a) pattern of consumption;
   (b) expectations held of the effect of alcohol on behaviour;
   (c) the physical, psychological and social characteristics of an individual;
   (d) the quantity of alcohol regularly consumed; and
   (e) prevailing social and economic conditions.
2. These five influences (a)–(e) are in dynamic interaction and therefore a multifactorial approach to causation is necessary.
3. A large number of serious physical illnesses and social and emotional problems are a direct result of alcohol over-use.
4. The prevalence of drinking problems is related to the level of per capita consumption.

The conclusion that has to be drawn is that 'alcoholics' are not a group with characteristics that distinguish them clearly from the rest of the population. Any person to whom alcohol is available and who regularly drinks large enough quantities will become subject to a number of physical disorders and social problems: and, as already noted, the rise in per capita consumption indicates that alcohol is becoming more readily available and that a proportion of the population is moving across the boundary from relatively safe to problem drinking.

Alcohol and its effects

Ethyl alcohol (ethanol), the form of alcohol active in wines, beers and spirit liquor, has a rapid and depressant effect on the central nervous system. This causes a reduction in the capacity of the individual to make reasoned judgements and to maintain normal controls. Most of us have some awareness of the disinhibiting effect of alcohol, which in its milder form releases us to be sociable and relaxed, and in its more extreme form causes foolhardy, boastful, provocative and even violent behaviour. Although alcohol is often thought of as a stimulant, it actually slows down our responses, and in very large quantities induces coma and death.

It is quite common for the regular over-user of alcohol to experience *blackouts*. A blackout does not involve a loss of consciousness and is more appropriately described as a period of amnesia. Usually the person is unable to remember the latter part of the previous evening's drinking or how he arrived home. He may check with friends to discover how he behaved during the period of which he has no memory. If he does he will find they noticed no particular difference in his behaviour at the time.

Many people have some experience of the gloomy feelings associated with being 'hung over', but when alcohol is taken regularly in large quantities its *depressant* effect produces a mood in which the person becomes 'prey to all sorts of doubts, miseries, suspicions and general gloom'. This state may be mistaken for a depressive illness and the significance of the person's drinking may be misunderstood or pass unnoticed (Royal College of Psychiatrists 1979).

The regular heavy drinker develops a degree of *tolerance* to alcohol. The mechanism by which this occurs is not clear, but it seems more likely to occur in people who drink heavily every day than in those whose drinking pattern is one of intermittent binges. The person who has achieved a high degree of tolerance may apparently function well with a high level of alcohol in the bloodstream, and often does not demonstrate typically drunken behaviour. In fact his ability to function may be impaired if his alcohol supply is temporarily cut. When this happens he becomes anxious and irritable and is only restored to 'normal' by resumption of drinking. A person in this situation is exhibiting characteristics of alcohol dependence.

Alcohol, like nicotine and the opiates, is a *drug of dependence* (addiction). This term is used to describe any substance that induces in the individual a compulsion to go on taking it on a continuous or periodic basis in order to experience its effects and sometimes to avoid the experience of discomfort which occurs in its absence (Royal College of Psychiatrists 1979). The capacity of alcohol to produce dependence seems to be less than that of heroin, since most of us drink in moderation without developing any compulsion (i.e. *craving*) whereas many people who take a little heroin seem to rapidly develop a need for regular and increasing supplies. Nevertheless, dependence on alcohol does develop and affects a much larger proportion of the population than dependence on heroin.

There are two components to dependence – psychological and physical. The individual may develop psychological dependence, in the form of reliance on alcohol for the relief of anxiety and the achievement of a sense of well-being, even though there may be no physical dependence. Physical dependence is demonstrated by the appearance of *withdrawal symptoms* in the absence of alcohol. These symptoms include tremor, especially of the hands, feelings of nausea, sweating, irritability and a heightened sense of anxiety. Withdrawal fits, which resemble major epileptic convulsions, may also occur. In the more extreme cases of withdrawal the individual may become apprehensive and fearful and experience auditory and/or visual hallucinations. The condition is then described as *delirium tremens*.

Psychological dependence is likely to cause a number of disagreeable problems (e.g. debt, caused because spending on alcohol takes precedence over paying the rent) and often seems to be a preliminary to physical dependence. The phrase *alcohol dependence syndrome* is increasingly used to describe the condition in which both psychological and physical dependence are present.

The alcohol dependence syndrome is presently defined by seven clinically observable characteristics (Edwards 1977).

1. The individual has narrowed the range of circumstances in which he drinks and has developed a regular drinking schedule. He will drink at regular intervals throughout the day and will arrange his activities to make sure he can easily reach alcohol at the times he is accustomed to drink. Differences between weekday and weekend drinking patterns will be much less marked than formerly.

2. Drinking will have taken precedence over other activities and interests. The individual will be paying rather little attention to the unpleasant consequences of his drinking and will show evidence of neglecting responsibility and surrendering values which previously strongly influenced his behaviour.

3. The person's tolerance for alcohol has increased, and he will be able to drink large quantities without appearing to be drunk.

4. Withdrawal symptoms have been experienced repeatedly. The symptoms likely to feature most commonly are heightened irritability and anxiety, tremor, nausea, retching and sweating (particularly at night).

5. The individual has discovered that further drinking provides relief from these symptoms within 30 minutes or so, and will regularly resume drinking to secure this relief. This has led to drinking at times other people think are inappropriate (e.g. early morning).

6. The person will be aware of sometimes feeling a compulsion to take a drink. He may describe this as feeling he must go on drinking once he has started. Alternatively he may feel compelled to seek a drink. This subjective feeling of craving may be as indicative of a psychological response to specific cues associated with drinking (e.g. passing a familiar public house) as it is of a physical response to a lowered alcohol level.

7. The symptoms described rapidly reappear after even quite prolonged periods of total abstinence.

Edwards suggests that his definition of the dependence syndrome takes account of the recent evidence challenging the existence of alcoholism as a disease without denying the relevance of the medical contribution to dealing with the symptoms described.

The term alcohol dependence syndrome is now frequently used in place of *alcoholism* and *alcohol addiction*. However, the Report of the Royal College of Psychiatrists (1979) chooses to use alcoholism to embrace 'every type of instance where someone is incurring serious or persistent disability as a result of his drinking, irrespective of dependence' (p. 10).

Edwards takes the view that it is helpful to distinguish alcohol induced symptoms from *alcohol related disabilities (problems)*. By the latter term he means the physical disorders, psychological and social problems that develop as a result of the over-use of alcohol. Edwards is probably right. It is very clear that alcohol related disabilities occur in people who do not demonstrate symptoms of dependence. It is also possible to become dependent and yet to experience few problems. High income, a comfortable home and supportive family, and a high level of personal and social skills all help to insulate the alcohol over-user from social problems; physical fitness and a large physique seem to afford some protection from physical illnesses associated with alcohol abuse. These factors do not, however, insure the individual against becoming alcohol dependent.

Factors affecting susceptibility

Some personal characteristics increase susceptibility to social and physical disability. For example, women are apparently much more likely than men to develop certain severe alcohol related illnesses (e.g. hepatitis); and recent twin and family studies suggest it is no longer possible to discount the genetic element in susceptibility to severe alcohol problems (Tsuang and Vandermey 1980). The nature of a person's work is also an influential factor. The catering industry and the production and retail of alcohol are well-known examples of work which carries a high risk of alcohol problems. Other high risk occupations include journalism, the merchant navy and the medical profession. Eight risk factors which collectively explain why such disparate occupations have high rates of alcohol related disability have been suggested (Plant 1977). They include the ready accessibility of alcohol during working hours, strong pressure amongst fellow workers to participate in heavy drinking, a job which regularly takes the person away from normal social and sexual relationships, freedom from supervision in the work place, a job which either offers affluence and high purchasing power or alternatively where low income may provide a 'particularly great need to use alcohol to dim harsh realities', a job situation in which the person's drinking can be covered up, work which provides special strains and stresses, and finally the possibility that high risk occupations may attract people who already drink excessively.

The pattern of drinking is a further influence on vulnerability to dependence and to alcohol problems. The person who drinks large quantities every day is susceptible to severe dependence and to liver dysfunction, but his pattern of continuous drinking makes him relatively unlikely to be found in a drunk and disorderly condition. In contrast the person whose drinking pattern is of weekend 'binges' may be less severely dependent and less prone to liver disease, but is more likely to be brought to court for drunkenness offences.

Although variation in susceptibility to specific symptoms and problems is apparent, it is clear that a *daily* intake equivalent to four pints of beer, or four doubles of spirits, or one bottle of wine, has to be regarded as the upper limit which it is safe for anyone to drink. It may be unwise in some circumstances to drink regularly even to this limit (e.g. during pregnancy).

The problems

Physical disorders

The death rate amongst those who have been diagnosed alcoholic has been shown to be more than twice that of the rest of the population (Adelstein and White 1976). The high rate for alcoholics is particularly apparent among deaths from accidents, poisoning and violence, and from diseases of the circulatory, respiratory and digestive systems. Alcohol abuse is demonstrably and dramatically threatening to life and clearly associated with a large number of incapacitating illnesses. It has been estimated that about 20 per cent of general hospital beds are taken up by people with alcohol related disability (Jarma and Kellett 1979).

Gastritis is probably the most commonly experienced alcohol induced disorder, and the acute abdominal discomfort it produces is a frequent cause of absence from work following drinking sprees. Beverage alcohol is a source of calories, and if taken in large quantities may be a cause of obesity. It is also a suppressant of appetite, and in circumstances where feelings of nausea and gastric pain ensuing from alcohol over-use interfere with normal eating patterns and where a person is so preoccupied with obtaining a regular supply of alcohol that little money or energy are available for preparing meals, malnutrition may occur. Peptic and duodenal ulcers are commonly a consequence of alcohol over-use, but it is not unusual for individuals to have surgery for these conditions and to remain unaware that their illness is associated with drinking, and consequently that a reduction in drinking is necessary if they are to remain well. Inflammation of the pancreas (pancreatitis) is an acute, painful condition and is frequently a consequence of a drinking spree. However, the most common serious alcohol induced illnesses of the digestive system are consequences of liver dysfunction.

Ethanol is metabolised in the liver, and when it is subjected to excessive quantities the liver becomes enlarged in an attempt to maintain the rate of metabolism. If excessive drinking continues fatty deposits develop and the liver may become inflamed (hepatitis). The incidence of this serious condition is a special cause for concern amongst women under 45 years who have been drinking heavily, as it has an earlier onset and a higher mortality rate among women than among men. If drinking continues scar tissue develops and the liver's capacity to function is seriously impaired. The person suffering from this liver cirrhosis may be bloated and yellow in appearance and may even be drowsy and confused. Oesophageal varices (distended veins at the lower end of the oesophagus) may develop as a consequence of cirrhosis and can haemorrhage suddenly and fatally. If the person with a cirrhotic liver becomes totally abstinent the disease is usually arrested, but when drinking continues the majority of sufferers die within five years.

By no means all over-users of alcohol develop a cirrhotic liver, but continuous heavy drinking makes the individual more susceptible to cirrhosis than does binge drinking. The recent trend in the UK towards a pattern of regular daily drinking in addition to traditional weekend drinking has increased the typical number of drinking occasions in a week for most people, and may be one reason for the rising incidence of cirrhosis (see Chapter 1).

Peripheral neuritis is another serious condition caused by alcohol over-use. It is characterised by loss of sensation in fingers and feet, and may be aggravated by poor diet. It is susceptible to treatment, although residual impairment may persist even when abstinence is maintained.

Two specific conditions affecting mental functioning have been identified as consequences of alcohol abuse. Wernicke's encephalopathy is a serious, rare illness requiring urgent treatment. It is characterised by unsteady gait, double vision, confusion, limited attention and sudden sleepiness. It is often the precursor of Korsakoff's psychosis, a condition typified by loss of memory of recent events, disorientation in time, a lack of insight and a tendency to invent stories to cover gaps in memory (confabulation). This is a severe form of dementia induced by many years of excessive drinking. Recent research has suggested that less severe, but significant, brain damage may commonly be present in younger people regularly drinking large quantities of alcohol (Lee *et al.* 1979).

Alcohol over-use significantly contributes to specific cardiac disorders, and respiratory illnesses, such as bronchitis, are common amongst over-users living in poor conditions. Drunkenness is a common cause of injuries caused by falls and burns, and problem drinkers amongst the elderly and women at home, as well as those on 'skid row', are subject to such accidents. Low birth weight and other foetal and neo-natal anomalies may be caused by heavy drinking during pregnancy (Sclare 1980).

One other problem which often requires urgent medical intervention should be noted. As many as 20 per cent of people who have been diagnosed as having serious alcohol problems have attempted suicide and an alarming proportion (8 per cent) succeed in killing themselves. (In the British population as a whole the suicide rate is approximately 10 per 100,000.) The problem drinker who commits suicide is more likely to be male than female and seems most prone to take his life when he is socially isolated and struggling with a situation that causes him to feel a sense of loss or failure (Ritson 1977). The fact that a person has attempted suicide on an earlier occasion should not be taken as an indication that it is simply attention-seeking behaviour. Those who have made the attempt often try again – and succeed.

The range of illness that follows from over-use of alcohol is very wide and includes seriously incapacitating and fatal conditions. However, it is neither appropriate nor effective to try to induce fear of the physical damage over-use of alcohol can cause. Problem drinkers cannot be helped by such a basically punitive approach. Nevertheless, it is necessary for the social worker to be aware of the serious nature of these alcohol induced illnesses since it is particularly important that realistic and practical information is presented to the problem drinker who has described such an illness, but has not understood its relationship to his drinking.

Psychological problems

The relatives of those with drinking problems often talk of the change in personality they feel has accompanied the increase in drinking. This chapter has already discussed some of the affective behaviour that contributes to this (see pp. 11–13). It has been noted that the person developing dependence on alcohol will become irritable and anxious as the level of alcohol in his system drops below that to which it has grown accustomed. Another type of irritability often develops when the person has taken so much alcohol that he demonstrates behaviour usually described as drunken. At such a time any minor disagreement may become the cause of a major and unpleasant argument, with the drunk person exhibiting wild and unfounded suspicions of his spouse and family. Sudden changes of mood may occur, and physical violence may explode during an argument. Alternatively, the individual may become suddenly morose and tearful. Life experience, as well as clinical observation, teach that it is not wise or fruitful to attempt to talk about any serious or controversial matter with someone who is drunk. It is certainly no time to raise questions about a person's drinking behaviour!

Guilt and remorse are frequently the dominant feelings of the person emerging from a period of excessive drinking. These emotions may be so preoccupying and stressful that the person makes a series of quite unrealistic promises about his future behaviour. There may be promises to never drink again, to make dramatic changes in behaviour at home, to meet whatever demands are made by spouse or employer. The promises will not – indeed cannot – be kept. Thus, a situation is created in which guilt and remorse again become dominant. This pattern tends to cause family members, employers and friends to regard the problem drinker as untrustworthy, uncaring or irresponsible, and the idea that the individual's personality has changed for the worse is reinforced by it.

The person who is regularly drinking excessively, and who is moving towards dependence on alcohol, is likely to be feeling that his drinking is becoming uncontrollable. He will find himself resorting to alcohol when he had not intended to drink and will become drunk on occasions when his intention had been moderate drinking. This chaotic situation in which autonomy and control are apparently lost is likely to increase the person's level of anxiety. Most of us are aware that alcohol temporarily relieves stress and the problem drinker quickly learns that another drink or two brings him rapid relief; that it also exacerbates his tendency to drink to excess may not be immediately clear to him. The person's anxiety may be heightened further by the marked reduction in libido which is a frequent consequence of regularly drinking to excess. For some, impotence will occur and may be associated with the intense and suspicious jealousy associated with drunkenness which has been described as the Othello syndrome.

The problem drinker, in attempting to reduce the tension in his social and personal relationships, may tell lies about his whereabouts, about the quantity he is regularly drinking, about the payment of bills, or about any other aspect of life that has potential for controversy. Alternatively he may be so confused or overwhelmed by the situation that he is unable to act with purpose or consistency.

Social problems

The social problems precipitated by over-use of alcohol are many and varied. They include some of the most common serious problems referred to social work agencies, although the degree to which they are experienced is always influenced by the social and financial circumstances of the individual and family concerned as well as by the quantity and pattern of drinking. The psychological problems and physical disorders described in the preceding sections of this chapter will exacerbate and even cause social problems. For example, repeatedly failing to appear at work on Monday morning because of withdrawal symptoms or gastritis will create difficulties. Or behaviour dominated by suspicion, irritability and lying may cause a spouse to seek a legal separation.

The most frequent and pervasive social problems for the over-user of alcohol are in his personal relationships. The marital partner is likely to experience fewer and fewer of the satisfactions he had expected from marriage and at the same time will find himself having to take over more and more of the role for which the drinking spouse previously took responsibility. A wife may find herself having to take more responsibility for paying bills and for providing income for the family; a husband may have to take more responsibility at home because the children are left uncared for and the washing and cleaning neglected. Whilst some families manage to survive unnoticed in these circumstances, many others may break down in familiar ways. There is some evidence that drinking frequently precedes violence between spouses, and it may commonly precede child abuse. It is obviously a factor in marital disharmony and may be the principal cause of disagreement, separation and divorce in some cases. Children are likely to be particularly vulnerable to harm in a family where one or both parents are drinking excessively. Young children, bewildered and frightened by what is happening, may demonstrate a wide range of disturbed and disturbing behaviour. Older children, with a clearer understanding of the cause of family difficulties, may experience considerable distress and feel forced to take responsibility for one or both parents. The premature maturity that is imposed on such children is often tenuous and the effort of sustaining it may seriously reduce the energy available for the normal and necessary activities of childhood and adolescence.

Other problems caused by over-use of alcohol have an impact on spouse and children. Regularly drinking large quantities of any form of beverage alcohol requires a good deal of expenditure, so for most families it will impose a strain on their budget. Often families find themselves in debt because money formerly allocated to the payment of routine bills has been spent on drink. Rent arrears may reach such proportions that eviction becomes likely; a building society may threaten to foreclose on a mortgage; gas or electricity may be disconnected. Financial difficulties may be exacerbated by difficulties at work. In addition to taking time off work because of the physical disorders alcohol has caused, the problem drinker is likely to be carrying out his job less competently than formerly. His judgements may be less reliable, his ability to solve problems or supervise other workers may be reduced, carelessness may cause him to have accidents when handling machinery and he may no longer be able to complete work within a reasonable time. Sometimes the person misses promotion because of his behaviour but manages to hold on to the job; sometimes incompetence will be the cause of redundancy.

Financial difficulties caused because too large a proportion of income has been spent on alcohol may lead to court appearances. These may be civil proceedings concerned with the payment of debts, but debts and the need for readily available supplies of alcohol may be a factor prompting involvement in criminal offences such as theft. Court appearance may also follow from behaviour more obviously associated with drinking, such as being found drunk and disorderly, creating a breach of the peace whilst drunk, and driving whilst under the influence of alcohol. Although it is possible for the commission of an alcohol related offence to be an isolated incident, its occurrence is generally recognised as an indicator of other alcohol problems. In any case it is appropriate to consider it here since the personal distress and social difficulties that arise from injuring or killing a pedestrian, losing a driving licence or participating in a drunken brawl may be severe. Offenders frequently claim diminished responsibility for their acts because they have been drinking before the commission of offences, and it seems to be common for crimes of violence to occur after the protagonist has been drinking. In many instances an ordinary evening at the pub will have been enough for the disinhibiting effect of alcohol and the reduction in self-control and capacity to reason to be great enough for a person to engage in impulsive, foolish or dangerous behaviour. However, sometimes violent and other serious offences are committed by people who are severely alcohol dependent.

The social problems associated with being tried and found guilty of an offence committted whilst under the influence of alcohol provide graphic illustrations of the reasons which make it important for a person to modify his drinking pattern whether or not he has been physically harmed by alcohol or demonstrates characteristics of the alcohol dependence syndrome.

A small number of over-users of alcohol appear in court very frequently indeed on charges of drunkenness. People in this situation are usually living in deprived conditions in hostels and shelters, or may be 'skippering'. The special difficulties of this group of problem drinkers have received a good deal of attention (Home Office 1971; Archard 1979; Cook 1980) and will be discussed in Chapters 4 and 5.

A person who has developed a degree of tolerance for alcohol, and for whom making sure of a regular supply of drink is becoming a preoccupation, is likely to have begun to develop a drinking pattern different from that of his friends and family. He may be seeking a drink at times of the day and on days of the week when they do not drink. He may also be drinking larger quantities than his companions on each drinking occasion. This change in drinking habits will reduce the pleasure of the sociable drinking in which the person previously engaged. One consequence of this is likely to be that he will increasingly drink by himself and sometimes will do so secretly. This social separation may be reinforced by a negative response to his increased drinking rate on the occasions when he joins with friends or spouse in the public house or at a party. A rejecting attitude will push the over-user into an isolated position and the isolated person, because few social pressures are imposed on his behaviour, may drink in an increasingly uncontrolled and unacceptable way. The situation will be made worse if the person's spouse becomes so critical and rejecting that the marital relationship is difficult to maintain. The person who reaches this point will have developed at least some of the characteristics of the alcohol dependence syndrome and will also be at the point at which he is at risk of social deterioration. He may already have lost interest in his appearance, dropped his standards of personal hygiene and become nocturnally incontinent. With increased social isolation the person has fewer opportunities to use or develop social skills, and his behaviour may become less and less acceptable in his normal social environment. Awareness of his vulnerability to extreme social isolation may only serve to increase the misery of the situation, thus perhaps encouraging rather than discouraging further drinking.

It is easy to appreciate that social deterioration will exacerbate difficulties between marital partners and make the disintegration of marriage and family more likely. Marital breakdown usually increases the problems of the alcohol abuser. When the marriage ends the person often finds it difficult to maintain a secure and comfortable home, and becomes less motivated to maintain personal appearance, to keep to a balanced diet or to hold down a job. Research studies suggest that the problem drinker who has lost his (or her) spouse is less likely to maintain sobriety after treatment than those whose marriages remain intact (Orford 1975).

Conclusion

The descriptive account of alcohol problems highlights the pervasive and disruptive influence of alcohol misuse. Physical disorders and psychological problems arising from over-use interact with the social situation, one social problem will prompt or escalate others and the people within the individual's social environment may suffer harm because of his drinking behaviour. It is crucial, if the person and his family are to be helped, that the social worker teases out these factors. Chapter 3 examines this process in more detail. First, however, the attitudes to alcohol and alcohol abuse held by social workers are considered.

3 Assessing Clients' Alcohol Problems

> When things go wrong and will not come right
> Though you do the best you can,
> When life looks black at the hours of night,
> A pint of plain is your only man.
>
> from *The Workman's Friend* by Flann O'Brien

The concluding section of Chapter 1 noted that the potential of primary care agents, such as social workers, for helping people with alcohol problems is now recognised (Advisory Committee on Alcoholism 1978) and that the methods of helping used by social workers, which require the active involvement of clients, are amongst those likely to be effective in bringing about appropriate changes in drinking behaviour. Chapter 2 has emphasised that social problems which are commonly the concern of social workers often result from alcohol abuse, and other indicators suggest that a substantial proportion of the clients of some social work agencies may have alcohol problems (Strathclyde 1978; Social Work Services Group 1979). It follows that it is relevant for social workers to consider alcohol misuse as a possible cause of difficulties in referrals made to them. However, the available evidence suggests that social workers in local authorities and probation and after-care do not readily recognise alcohol problems, nor regard these problems as aspects of the clients' situation in which they can appropriately intervene (Robinson 1976; Shaw *et al.* 1978). It is necessary to examine this situation before going on to detailed discussion of the process of assessing clients with alcohol problems.

Social worker orientation to alcohol and alcohol abuse

The reports of the Maudsley Alcohol Pilot Project (Cartwright *et al.* 1975; 1977) show that the social workers surveyed were not well informed about alcohol dependence nor about alcohol related disorders and that they were uncertain how to apply social work skills and methods to these problems. These findings seem to be confirmed by discussion with practitioners in both statutory and voluntary agencies – social workers do not often think of psychological and social problems such as intense jealousy, marital discord, debt and evidence of stress in a child as being direct consequences of alcohol use, nor have they linked alcohol use to medical problems such as gastritis and the social problems that follow.

Opportunities to learn about alcohol misuse are becoming available to social workers, but the training and career development of many practitioners has offered little understanding of the subject and this seems to have a number of consequences for current practice.

1. In the absence of factual information social workers have tended to hold the common stereotype of 'alcoholic' (Cartwright *et al.* 1975). The stereotype is of a down and out person who is hopelessly addicted, and because it is only these problem drinkers the social worker recognises, he fails to appreciate that they constitute perhaps 2 per cent of the total of people with alcohol problems and that whilst they often exhibit drunken behaviour they may not be severely dependent.

2. Social workers who hold views close to the stereotype tend to perceive alcohol abuse as a chronically difficult to treat illness (Cartwright *et al.* 1975) and social workers holding an illness model of alcoholism seem reluctant to explore clients' use of alcohol, even where they are well placed to do so. They tend to rely on medical specialists to establish the existence of alcohol problems. However, access to specialist medical help is usually through general practitioners, who often do not associate the complaints presented to them with alcohol over-use (Wilkins 1974; Shaw *et al.* 1978). Alcohol problems frequently remain hidden in spite of attendance at surgeries and out-patient clinics; reliance on medical intervention as the means of identification is not appropriate.

3. It is still a commonly held view in our society that most people with alcohol problems are unlikely ever to change their drinking behaviour and social workers often take this pessimistic position (Cartwright *et al.* 1975). Practitioners who think over-users of alcohol are incorrigible or 'hopeless causes' will not put energy into encouraging change, especially when confronted by a morose or guilty person who is overwhelmed by the chaos resulting from his uncontrolled drinking and lacks confidence in his capacity to regain control. However, the notions that people with drinking problems never change their behaviour and that they have to reach rock bottom before improvement is possible have been thoroughly dis-

credited. The evidence that change is possible is irrefutable, and it is easier to achieve at an early stage in the development of alcohol problems.

4. Excessive use of alcohol by clients who do not fit the stereotype seems to be perceived by social workers as a *response* to circumstances rather than the *cause* of them. Alcohol over-use may be described as a response to personal problems, or it may be thought to be conformity to the norm within a particular neighbourhood or group. The tendency is to conclude that alcohol over-use will cease as problems are resolved and that it is improper to discuss drinking behaviour with clients whose social millieu includes regular heavy drinking, as this would imply an inappropriately judgemental attitude to socio-cultural norms. Such conclusions fail to take account of the harm resulting from alcohol misuse. They also place the social worker in a position from which it is difficult to grasp the significance of complaints about drinking by a marriage partner and which inhibits the checking of facts with the person whose drinking is criticised. When drinking behaviour is a causative factor ignoring it will not make it go away; indeed further and increasingly serious problems will frequently develop. The following example* illustrates the point:

> The Henchard family incurred serious debts. Rent arrears were such that there was a real possibility of eviction; sums were owed to a local grocer and payments to hire purchase companies were in arrears; the gas supply to the house was about to be cut. The social worker arranged a grant of money to ensure the family was not made homeless. This was followed by a period during which Mr and Mrs Henchard were supported in their efforts to pay off outstanding debts and help was given with budgeting. The social worker knew that Mr Henchard sometimes came home late on Friday after spending the evening at the local pub and that Mrs Henchard was very critical of this behaviour. She thought it understandable that Mr Henchard should want the occasional night out and expected his wife's criticism to cease once the stress produced by the financial difficulties was reduced. Three months after the case had been closed, the family was referred back to the social worker: there were more serious debts and Mrs Henchard was threatening to leave her husband. Further enquiry by the social worker elicited that Mr Henchard had been drinking

* All names have been changed.

heavily on several evenings each week, and that he frequently failed to go to work on Monday because of the after-effects of his weekend binges. He had been drinking in this pattern for more than a year and during this period had become less and less interested in his home and children, and increasingly bad tempered and critical of his wife.

Mr Henchard had already established a harmful drinking pattern at the time of the social worker's initial contact and reduction in stress and the early experience of success in dealing with the debts did nothing to alter this pattern. His drinking had been seen only as one of the background features against which the financial problems figured. But if alcohol related problems are to be prevented and alcohol dependence arrested it is necessary to assess the possibility that alcohol use is a causative factor in the difficulties experienced by clients.

5. Social workers who have rather little knowledge about alcohol use and abuse may have had little stimulus to reflect on their own drinking behaviour (or on their total abstinence). Many practitioners are young (in 1977 an estimated 40 per cent were under 30) and have recent experience of the student culture, so may be included in that segment of the population known to drink frequently and sometimes in considerable quantity. It may be very difficult for them to feel comfortable about discussing alcohol use with clients and to distinguish clearly between social and harmful drinking.

6. Social workers with little knowledge or experience of alcohol misuse who have been promoted to posts as team leaders and area officers or assistant chief probation officers are unlikely to accord priority to clients' alcohol problems. They may not even think of these as being primarily the concern of social work and will have little appreciation of the extent to which clients suffer alcohol problems or of the capacity of social work intervention for solving them. Furthermore, they are unlikely to offer support to practitioners who are trying to give attention to alcohol misuse, or provide the kind of supervision that enables practitioners to successfully apply their knowledge and skill in work with clients who have alcohol problems. The absence of support and supervision from senior staff may have a particular impact in agencies where the pressure of work is such that the primary focus has to be on urgent problems and short-term work and where work-

load and agency structure inevitably limit opportunities to consider whether long-term resolution of such difficulties as debt, family violence or truancy may be dependent on a change in drinking behaviour by one family member.

This discussion has emphasised the necessity of changing the orientation of practitioners to alcohol use and abuse. It argues that a sound knowledge base and agency policies and practice which facilitate active, early intervention with clients who present alcohol problems are necessary aids to the change. The range of clients harmed by misuse of alcohol is wide and the skilful application of social work methods can enable many to resolve their alcohol related difficulties.

The importance of assessment

It is only when the details of the drinking pattern and its consequences emerge that it is possible to estimate the extent of the change in drinking behaviour that may be advisable, and the impact that maintaining the change will have on the person, on his family and social environment. Only when the details are clear will the worker be able to assess whether the person is seriously dependent and in need of medical help; to comment about the advisability of developing the goal of abstinence; or to estimate the degree to which the individual experiences social pressures that make a reduction in drinking difficult.

The process of assessment also helps the client and those significant in his environment to move towards recognition of the relationship between drinking and the problems they are experiencing. If their understanding is increased through the processes of assessment and recognition, their ability to take action to ease the situation may also be enhanced. This may be especially important for the person whose spouse, or employer, is angry and rejecting because of his unacceptable behaviour. Increased awareness of the problem will help them to provide an environment in which the person is supported in his attempt to regain control and competence.

Although it will not always be possible at the initial interview to fully assess the significance of alcohol use to the client's problems, it is important to try to complete this assessment early in the contact.

Establishing the significance of alcohol use

Social workers based in ATUs and in specialist voluntary agencies will regularly be referred people already known to have alcohol related problems, as will those probation officers whose primary concern is with habitual drunken offenders and homeless ex-prisoners. However, the great majority of social workers will be presented with clients referred for quite other reasons (e.g. the Henchard family – see p. 26), whose alcohol use has not previously been considered to be significant. This means that, unlike specialist workers, most social workers have to start the screening process from the beginning and that frequently they will be faced with resistance by the client to considering alcohol use to be a problem. It will help if the worker holds in his mind the range of problems (outlined in Chapter 2) which are known to be frequently alcohol related. He will then be equipped to pick up clues that alcohol mis-use may be a feature. This is a necessary preliminary to raising the issue with the client. The following example will help to illustrate the relevance of keeping in mind the possibility that the client's drinking behaviour may be important.

> A local authority social worker working two days a week in a group practice received a referral from a general practitioner. Mrs Charmond, a widow of 45, had been to see the general practitioner three times in the previous four months. On two occasions she had asked for 'pills to make me sleep', but had not been able to explain fully her need for them. The general practitioner understood she had difficulty getting to sleep and that she 'feels awful' on waking. On one recent appearance at the surgery she had quite severe bruising and lacerations to her face and legs. She said her cat had been in the way and she had tripped on the stone steps leading to her flat. The general practitioner was puzzled about Mrs Charmond. He had known her for some years and thought of her as a competent and lively person, although she appeared dejected now. He had prescribed a sedative after her last visit to the surgery, but did not want to repeat the prescription. He asked that the social worker try to investigate Mrs Charmond's situation and her need of further help.

This referral makes no mention of alcohol use: it had not occurred to the general practitioner to consider it. The facts might indicate a depressive illness, reactive to some aspect of Mrs Charmond's situation. Her age and her widowhood, as well as the difficulty in sleeping and her dejected appearance might support this. However, there are some aspects of the picture which might not be consistent with depression. Mrs Charmond has recently come to the surgery rather frequently, yet the general practitioner is still unclear what is the matter. She has not described herself as tired or depressed, but as feeling 'awful' (which seems to imply 'ill') first thing in the morning. Furthermore, this normally competent, lively woman has recently hurt herself quite badly in a clumsy fall. Excessive drinking could be the explanation, but there is only enough information here to raise that possibility in the worker's mind. The initial contact with Mrs Charmond demonstrates the means by which necessary information can be elicited and highlights some of the tension and difficulties raised by the assessment process.

> The social worker made an appointment to see Mrs Charmond. He noted a number of additional points available to him before his conversation with her began. Mrs Charmond was more than half-an-hour late for her two o'clock appointment and her appearance was rather dishevelled. Her quite expensive clothes were crumpled and her hair was untidy. She seemed flustered.

These non-verbal indicators are important as they give a picture of disorganisation, but not necessarily of depression. The picture could be consistent with over-use of alcohol, but other explanations (e.g. a change in Mrs Charmond's financial situation, or a level of anxiety which is so high that it is incapacitating) are equally possible.

> After introducing himself the social worker explained the general practitioner's concern that Mrs Charmond may have some difficulties that are causing her to be upset; he added that he would like to be of help to her. The worker aimed to focus first on Mrs Charmond's perception of her situation and encouraged her to give him a detailed description, although she seemed reluctant to begin.
>
> *Mrs Charmond:* I've told the doctor I can't sleep. I need pills to help me. That is all there is to it.
>
> *Social worker:* Yes, Dr B. told me you have pills to help you just now, but I'm sure he doesn't think it a good idea for you to rely on them for a permanent solution. Perhaps it would be helpful to try to find out why you are having difficulty in sleeping. If we understood that it might be possible to find a permanent solution that made the pills unnecessary. Having disturbed nights is very wearying and unpleasant. I wonder if it has been a trouble to you for a long time?
>
> *Mrs Charmond:* It seems like a long time – months anyway.
>
> *Social worker:* Can you remember when it started?

Mrs Charmond: Well, I used to worry a lot about my job. I had a really interesting job and enjoyed it very much, but the responsibility used to make me worry sometimes.
Social worker: You speak of it in the past - did you give it up?
Mrs Charmond: (became quite tense and agitated at this point, but continued) There was a dreadful upset, and after that I was transferred to another department. It's not the same; the people there don't want me working with them.
Social worker: It sounds as though the old job gave you pleasure and satisfaction as well as worry.
Mrs Charmond: Yes, it made me feel I was doing something worthwhile. The departmental managers often came to me for advice on administrative matters.
Social worker: Your job must have meant a lot to you then.
Mrs Charmond: Yes, it did, I suppose after my husband died I put a lot into it. I don't have any family and I don't bother with company these days. I suppose the job grew in importance. Then, when I was moved I felt miserable. That was about six months ago.
Social worker: What's the new job like?
Mrs Charmond: Oh, it's all right I suppose. Just a different department - not so interesting and I know the people there don't like me.
Social worker: What makes you think that?
Mrs Charmond: They heard all about the trouble in my old department. A mistake was made and I got the blame. That's why I was transferred. Now everyone gossips about me.

Alcohol has not been mentioned. However, the details that are emerging could suggest an underlying alcohol problem. Mrs Charmond has indicated that she has withdrawn from social activity recently, that she may have made an uncharacteristic but serious error at work, and that she is regarded with some suspicion by her workmates. It is not going to be possible to assess the relevance of drink unless it is raised directly and the worker will probably have to take the initiative to introduce the subject. This must be done carefully. A too tentative or oblique reference will indicate to the client that it is a difficult and frightening topic, and thus discourage him from being frank; too confronting an approach may put the client into a defensive position or provoke his anger. The subject must be introduced clearly and confidently, yet without implying that judgements are being made. In Mrs

Charmond's case the worker brought the conversation back to her withdrawal from company, since he thought this might be a significant aspect of the situation. After hearing from her about the church and social activities in which she used to be involved the worker asked how she now spent her spare time.

Mrs Charmond: I just go home and watch the TV.
Social worker: Do you sometimes feel like going out – for a drink perhaps?
Mrs Charmond: I might have a glass of wine at home.
Social worker: Do you ever ask any friends in?
Mrs Charmond: No, I've lost touch with my old friends.
Social worker: I wonder if you ever feel like finishing the bottle of wine yourself.
Mrs Charmond: Well, I do enjoy a good bottle of wine. And I think a few glasses help me get to sleep. It makes me feel more relaxed – sometimes I think it does me more good than an evening meal.

The social worker now knows that Mrs Charmond regularly drinks on her own, but it is not clear how often or how much. Mrs Charmond has hinted that she may sometimes prefer to drink than to eat. It is necessary to explore her drinking pattern in more precise detail and to keep in mind that the sedative drug that has been prescribed may be potentiating the effects of alcohol.

Social worker: Perhaps you prefer to have your main meal at lunch time.
Mrs Charmond: I go to a nice pub at lunch time. I have a snack there.
Social worker: Do you have a drink as well?
Mrs Charmond: I might have a glass or two.
Social worker: Of wine?
Mrs Charmond: I usually have a whisky at lunch time.
Social worker: Do you usually have two lunch time whiskies as well as a few glasses of wine in the evening?
Mrs Charmond: It makes me feel good.
Social worker: Yes, I can see you enjoy it. Would you normally drink that amount every day?
Mrs Charmond: Most days. Why not?
Social worker: Well, I am just beginning to wonder whether some of your sleep difficulties and your early morning problems might be related to your drinking.

Mrs Charmond: Here we go again. Just because I enjoy a drink you start leaping to conclusions. You people are all the same!

The social worker is managing to discover a good deal of information about Mrs Charmond's drinking pattern. However, he still does not know exactly how important a part alcohol plays in the situation. He feels he must introduce the possibility that it is significant, and does so at the first opportunity. Understandably, Mrs Charmond shows anger, but even in her angry response she indicates that the possibility that she is over-using alcohol has been raised before. The social worker must now find a way of pursuing the topic without increasing her anger and defensiveness. It will be important for him to make sure he discusses alcohol use in a way that shows its relevance to the problems Mrs Charmond is currently experiencing.

Social worker: Leaping to conclusions?
Mrs Charmond: You've decided I'm a drunk. I'm used to it, everyone talking behind my back, saying how awful it is for a woman to drink. Those dreadful people at the church said it, and the people at work gossip too. And you ask why I don't go out or have people in! All I get is accusations and people cutting me dead. They are all so narrow-minded.

Once again, Mrs Charmond has given important information in her angry, hurt outburst. The social worker must find ways of keeping this information available in the interview without becoming part of the uncaring, punishing environment Mrs Charmond feels is surrounding her.

Social worker: I'm sorry that people seem to have been unkind. Perhaps it all makes you feel it is better to be on your own with a bottle of wine.
Mrs Charmond: That's true, sometimes I do.
Social worker: Lots of people think a drink is a comfort when they have been hurt or are feeling lonely. The only difficulty is that sometimes they grow to rely so much on drink for providing comfort that things get out of hand and they turn to it for help with all sorts of little stresses and strains that are a normal part of life.
Mrs Charmond: Well, I suppose I do tend to take a drink if I am upset or anything – but I don't think that is wrong.
Social worker: I don't think it is wrong either, but it may create problems instead of solving them.

Mrs Charmond: How could it do that?

The social worker has managed to keep an appropriate focus on alcohol, and has done so in a way that is relevant to Mrs Charmond's situation. He has been careful not to reinforce any idea she may have that he will be judgemental or 'narrow-minded' and has given Mrs Charmond sufficient reassurance to make it possible for her to ask for basic information. This enables him to show knowledgeable concern at the point when the client seems receptive. At this point it is most important to avoid bombarding the client with too much information. Furthermore, it is still not clear how significant a cause of her difficulties Mrs Charmond's drinking is, so the worker must be careful not to imply more than he actually knows and to present information in a way which encourages her to discuss its relevance and to give more details of her drinking pattern. It seemed appropriate to concentrate on information which relates to Mrs Charmond's acknowledged difficulties, that is, sleep disturbance, feeling ill in the early morning, irritability and difficulty in concentrating in the morning, and the attitudes of her former friends. As soon as the worker mentioned the symptoms of nausea and shakiness that can occur, Mrs Charmond chimed in:

Mrs Charmond: It's true, I do feel shaky. My hands tremble and I am shaky inside somehow. It's an awful feeling. It puts me off my breakfast. But I think it's my nerves that make me feel like that. I get so miserable and I don't see the point of another day of backbiting at the office. I don't really want to go to work – that's what makes me feel so ill. Taking a drink helps me to face it all.

Mrs Charmond has an alternative explanation for her symptoms. Although it is very likely that her shakiness and inability to eat her breakfast are consequences of her drinking, the worker cannot be sure about this. In any case it would almost certainly provoke a negative response in Mrs Charmond if he argued the point. A helpful outcome is very much more likely if he can demonstrate an ability to listen to her explanation and show interest in understanding what brought her to it. In using this approach the worker gained new and important information without increasing Mrs Charmond's defensiveness or provoking shame.

Social worker: Has anything happened to make you think a drink helps you?

> *Mrs Charmond:* Well, sometimes I have a little glass of whisky about 11 o'clock and it settles my stomach. I feel I can face the day after that, and I get on better with my work.
> *Social worker:* Do you often take a drink at that time?
> *Mrs Charmond:* Quite often, I suppose; most days really.
> *Social worker:* I suppose it's easy enough to slip out to a local pub at opening time.
> *Mrs Charmond:* Oh, I don't leave the office. I keep a little bottle in my desk – then I know I can have another sip if things get too awful later on.

It is now clear that on 'most days' Mrs Charmond has an unusually high intake of alcohol – one or more glasses of whisky in the office, a further two whiskies at lunch time and several glasses of wine in the evening. This is above the daily intake accepted as the safe upper limit (see Chapter 1). Her drinking is solitary, sometimes she has a drink instead of eating, and she seems to drink in the morning to reduce withdrawal symptoms. It is very likely that her difficulties at work are associated with her over-use of alcohol and probable that physical illness will ensue if drinking is maintained at this level. The worker has established that alcohol is a significant factor in Mrs Charmond's situation, although it is likely that in this first interview Mrs Charmond has not described the full extent of her drinking. He has enough information on which to begin his assessment, and to have some idea of the short-term goals he and the general practitioner could most usefully pursue. Before moving on to discussion of goals, however, the worker needs to be in a position to estimate his client's current capacity to make and maintain a decision to reduce alcohol use.

The client's capacity for change

Capacity and motivation to make and maintain the decision to change behaviour will be dependent on a number of factors:

1. the client's understanding of the reasons that make a reduction in alcohol use advisable;
2. acceptance of the validity of those reasons;
3. the advantages perceived to result from a reduction in drinking;
4. the perceived disadvantages resulting from reducing drinking;
5. the ability of the client to develop ways of coping with stress and discomfort that do not include alcohol use;

6. the ability to find alternative and satisfying activities to those previously associated with drinking;
7. the degree of support and help available in the client's family, work and social situation; and
8. appropriate help from social work agencies, the health service and volunteer and self-help organisations.

Clearly it is neither possible nor appropriate to explore all these factors in the initial interview. It is, however, particularly important to give attention to the first four at initial assessment.

Unless the client understands that his drinking pattern has been assessed as harmful (factor 1) and accepts the evidence on which the assessment has been made (factor 2), he will not be motivated to change his behaviour. Since ultimately only the client has control over whether or not he has an alcoholic drink on each occasion that one is available, his commitment to change his behaviour is especially crucial. The degree of commitment and its maintenance will be dependent on the third factor – the client's perception of the advantages that would accrue if alcohol use was reduced or totally abandoned – and on the balance between this and the potential disadvantages of reducing alcohol intake (factor 4).

It is important that the worker engages the client positively in the process of identifying and assessing his alcohol problems, that he gives relevant factual information and that the client is free to question and explore the issues raised, if motivation for change is to be maximised. The worker should show confidence in any information he gives and be able to dispel any myths about alcohol use in which the client demonstrates a belief (e.g. only spirit drinkers become alcohol dependent). It will be necessary for the worker to show he is knowledgeable without overwhelming or alienating the client. It will not be helpful to catalogue every aspect of the client's circumstances which is affected by alcohol use. In Mrs Charmond's case, for example, many aspects of her situation and appearance (her clumsy fall, her lateness, her dishevelled appearance, her difficulties at work, her rejection by people at church), are probably explained by her over-use of alcohol. However, demonstrating that this is the case would be a long process and one likely to increase Mrs Charmond's resistance to using help and advice. It is more productive for the worker to begin with the matters that seem of current importance to the client and to introduce further issues only when they become relevant. Some issues may not be discussed until weeks, or even months, after the initial contact.

Once the worker is clear alcohol over-use is a significant issue for Mrs Charmond he focuses his comments on her feelings about her job. This seems appropriate as she has already indicated that work had been an area of her life in which she was interested and had experienced personal success.

> *Social worker:* I'm sorry things often seem so bad at work. From what you have said I think you must hold a quite senior position and in the past you obviously found it very satisfying. You were well thought of too. Recently things have been very different for you and I can see how miserable you are about that.
>
> *Mrs Charmond:* Nothing ever seems to go right for me these days. But, it's true . . . people used to tell me I was good at my job.
>
> *Social worker:* Well, I think you might be able to get back to that position. You see, from what you have told me about the way you feel in the mornings and about the way another drink seems to make you feel better, I am pretty sure that many of your problems are actually caused by drinking, not solved by it.
>
> *Mrs Charmond:* I don't see how you could come to that conclusion at all. I've told you a glass of wine helps me to relax of an evening and a sip of whisky settles my nerves – helps me to face the day.

Although the social worker has been rather direct here, he has managed to convey his understanding of some of Mrs Charmond's unhappiness and has also encouraged her to be hopeful by indicating that she could again achieve the kind of satisfactions she formerly gained from her work. Mrs Charmond is not convinced that her drinking is a cause of difficulties, but is still engaged in the discussion and able to listen to what is being said. The worker must now find a way of offering factual information which avoids making it so frightening that it is rejected.

> *Social worker:* Yes, it is true that a couple of drinks help us to feel more relaxed. Difficulties only really arise when a person is taking four, or five, or more drinks each day. At that level of regular drinking a person is likely to be harmed by alcohol in some way or another. And the kind of problems you have described – sleep disturbances, early morning shakiness and tension and feeling gloomy and miserable – are common consequences of drinking the kind of quantities you regularly take.

Mrs Charmond: You are wrapping it up a bit, but I think you are telling me I'm a common drunk – headed in the same direction as those dreadful people you see sprawling in the Public Gardens.

Mrs Charmond showed a good deal of distress at this point. Her eyes filled with tears and she lifted her bag as if she might break off the interview. At such a moment the level of tension is high for both the worker and the client and it is important that the social worker, whilst providing appropriate reassurance for the client, keeps the issue of drinking available for further exploration.

Social worker: No, I am not telling you that you are a common drunk. But I am saying that I think you may have become dependent on alcohol. Alcohol is rather like tobacco in the way you can get so into the habit of using it that you become quite dependent on it. It isn't quite so easy to become dependent on drink as on tobacco, it is true.

Mrs Charmond: Now you are saying I'm an alcohol addict. Well, that's it. There is no hope for me then!

The susceptibility of clients with alcohol problems to feelings of despair was described in Chapter 2, and Mrs Charmond provides an example of the powerfulness of such feelings at the moment when she is struggling with basic information about her circumstances. If the social worker holds the pessimistic feelings about clients with alcohol problems described at the beginning of this chapter he will be unable to provide the realistic appraisal and reassurance the client needs to support any decision to take action to reduce drinking. The social worker interviewing Mrs Charmond made an appropriately positive statement.

Social worker: On the contrary, there are lots of reasons to be hopeful. Many people who have experienced difficulties that were caused by their drinking have found that once they have cut down the amount they drink, or given it up altogether, their health has improved and their energy for getting involved at work and with friends has increased. You have obviously been very successful in the past – at work and in your social life – I think you could be as successful again.

Mrs Charmond: Things are bad now, but I'm afraid they would be worse if I didn't have a glass of something to keep me going.

The client is not convinced. For most people with alcohol problems the prospect of life without the 'comfort' of a drink seems bleak. This is entirely understandable. Clients are frequently using alcohol to provide relief from stress and, if they are dependent, to ensure that withdrawal symptoms are kept at bay. A great deal of their time and attention is focused on drinking, so giving up or even reducing it may raise anxieties about how the available hours are to be filled (see factors 5 and 6 on pp. 35–6). It is not surprising that clients look for ways of avoiding the conclusion that beverage alcohol is causing more problems than it is solving. However, the social worker should persist in gently pointing out the reality; it would be inappropriate for him to become discouraged by the client's avoidance and denial.

> *Social worker:* Yes, I can see that is how it seems. Your shakiness in the morning helps me to understand that. You see, I think there is little doubt those awful morning feelings are caused because the level of alcohol in your body has dropped below what it has grown accustomed to. Once you have topped up with a whisky or two you feel better, although I expect sometimes when you have had another couple of whiskies at lunch time and a bit more when you get back to the office, you have difficulty in coping at work in the afternoon.
> *Mrs Charmond:* Oh, that's true. It's awful!
> *Social worker:* Well, there are quite a lot of people who have similar difficulties to yours.
> *Mrs Charmond:* But, I'm often in trouble because I'm not getting through the work that has to be done.

In saying this Mrs Charmond is accepting that at least one of her problems is a direct consequence of her drinking. It is likely that other people had already suggested drink was interfering with her competence, but on this occasion she states it is so herself and thus makes it possible to explore how the problem might be resolved. Once this stage in the assessment process has been reached some short-term goals can be discussed with the client.

> *Mrs Charmond:* (became quite tearful but continued to talk) I used to be able to do the work and cope with all sorts of emergencies. Now the work comes piling in and I just don't seem able to think out how to tackle it. Then people complain that important decisions are being held up because of me. Sometimes I just sit there feeling confused and miserable.
> *Social worker:* It sounds as if you are in an awful situation. I can

quite see why you are so worried and upset by it. Are there any times when it seems better?

Mrs Charmond: Well, as I told you a whisky does settle me mid-morning and then I can get on for a while.

Social worker: How about the afternoons?

Mrs Charmond: Oh, it just goes from bad to worse as the afternoon wears on, but a sip out of the bottle in my desk makes me feel better for a while.

Social worker: You know, everything you are telling me fits exactly with the experience of many people who have become dependent on alcohol. I am sure things would improve at work if you could come to a decision to stop drinking altogether, for a while at least.

Mrs Charmond: You seem very confident . . . I can't go on as I am just now. Perhaps I should try it for a while . . . but it would be like giving up my most trusted friend.

Social worker: Yes, it would be hard, but Dr B. and I can offer some help that would make it easier.

Mrs Charmond: What can you possibly do?

The social worker went on to suggest that he talk to the general practitioner and arrange a time the next day when the three of them could meet to plan how she could stop drinking altogether for a while; Mrs Charmond agreed to this. The worker explained that in the first few days of abstinence she might feel quite poorly. He indicated that Dr B. would probably want to carry out some medical checks and would see that medical and nursing care were available to ensure the discomfort of any withdrawal symptoms was reduced to the minimum. He went on:

Social worker: In a few days you will be up and about again and able to return to work. I realise it may be difficult to go back and that you may feel like having a drink again, but you and I can work out together how to cope with any difficulties that arise. I can arrange to see you quite often at first, and I will give you my phone number so that you can get in touch easily if any unexpected difficulties occur. Once you feel able to cope confidently at work we can review the situation again.

The social worker is careful not to minimise the difficulty Mrs Charmond will have in becoming abstinent and handling her work satisfactorily. However, he also conveys hope that she can manage it and reassures her that support and help will be available. It is particularly important to recognise the difficulty likely to arise in the first weeks of abstinence and the worker is careful to make sure Mrs Charmond knows she can rely on frequent contact with him during that period. He indicates the appropriateness of returning to work quickly and in his last comment emphasises the importance of reviewing the sutuation after a period of abstinence. He has already elicited Mrs Charmond's social isolation as well as a hint that she was much more gregarious earlier in her life. It may be that once her difficulties at work are resolved and she is feeling physically fitter, she will become more aware of her loneliness and need help in reducing it.

The method of assessment

It is clear from the analysis of the first contact with Mrs Charmond that the knowledge and skills employed are those the social worker would expect to use in the course of the initial assessment of any newly referred client. The worker focuses the discussion so that relevant information can emerge without leaving the client feeling too exposed and vulnerable; he provides realistic reassurance yet appropriately pursues sensitive issues he perceives to be central to the client's situation; he is direct, but not assertive; he is responsive to the client's questions and ready to listen to her; he helps her to go further by using what he knows (in this case about alcohol misuse); he shares his assessment with her and negotiates agreement about what action to take in the short term. However, there are some aspects of the assessment of clients with alcohol related problems which are different in emphasis, although not in kind. These relate to the view of alcohol misuse currently held in our society and to specific consequences of drinking large quantities of beverage alcohol.

1. The client's understanding of the effects of having large quantities of ethanol in his body is likely to be meagre and consequently the worker's ability to give straightforward factual information relevant to the specific client's circumstances is important. The client should not be overwhelmed by too much (often alarming) information as he will become resistant to using help or deny the relevance of alcohol. The worker needs skill in selecting the information it is appropriate to give and in presenting it clearly in language the client understands. It may be helpful to begin with the fact that many other people regularly drink very large quantities and experience similar problems as a result. Clients often find this information reassuring.

It will usually be plain to the worker that some of the matters it is relevant to discuss will increase the level of tension in the interview when they are raised. The social worker may have to make a conscious effort to resist a wish in himself to avoid the significant issues and thus escape the feeling of anxiety increased tension brings.

2. Two factors make it important that the detail of clients' personal history and of the origins of their use of alcohol do not dominate the initial assessment interview. The clients' predisposition to feeling shame and despair and to denial of the relevance of alcohol use make it likely that exploration of all the possible alcohol related problems and insistent searching for the 'causes' of alcohol misuse will increase the rate of negative responses in clients. Secondly, clients are better able to make use of detailed examination of their drinking behaviour once they have accepted the importance of changing it.

The assessment interview should focus on establishing the relationship between alcohol use and immediate problem(s) the client would like to resolve. This is likely to increase the client's motivation as it will give him something in the area with which he has asked for help. Other alcohol related difficulties can be examined later. For this reason the social worker interviewing Mrs Charmond did not attempt to discover whether her transfer to a less interesting job, the loss of her friends and withdrawal from social activity were direct consequences of her drinking. All of these aspects of her situation were recorded, however, so that the worker could keep them in mind in his subsequent discussions with Mrs Charmond.

3. It will be important that the social worker does not reinforce any punitive or despairing view of alcohol problems that may be held by the client and significant people in his social milieu. The worker's ability to be both realistic about the seriousness of the problems and appropriately optimistic about their resolution is likely to be very important in influencing clients to use help and advice. If the worker is to be appropriately optimistic he needs sound knowledge of the services that are available to clients with alcohol problems and of the methods of work he can most effectively use in his direct work with them. The chapter which follows outlines the available services and Chapters 5 and 6 focus on social work methods.

4 The Nature and Extent of Provision

The variety of alcohol problems (see Chapter 2) and the heterogeneity of those who over-use alcohol make it important that each client is offered the help appropriate to his needs. The importance of the availability of a range of different services is emphasised further by the fact that each client may require different types of service at different stages in the process of identifying and resolving his alcohol problems. There are three phases to this process:

1. At initial contact some people will present acute conditions requiring urgent attention. These include accidental injury, the consequences of violence, serious withdrawal symptoms, hepatitis, suicide attempts and imminent eviction. At this point the need is for services which alleviate the acute problems rather than those concerned with drinking behaviour, although in most of these circumstances temporary cessation of drinking will be crucial to the immediate relief of the urgent problem and will be imposed on clients by medical and nursing staff.
2. Once the acute phase has passed services designed to facilitate change in drinking behaviour will be required. For some people (e.g. Mrs Charmond) this will be the first phase of the helping process.
3. When sobriety has been established, most clients will need help with longer term issues in their social and personal situation.

The importance of matching services with the changing requirements of clients suggests that the social worker should be well informed about the range of available services in his locality and should work in collaboration with other agencies. The importance of a good information base and of collaborative working is reinforced by four additional factors:

1. In many instances the social worker will be the first person to identify the client's alcohol problems and will undertake the initial assessment of the client's need for help (Mrs Charmond provides an example). Only when he knows what services are available and what it is realistic to expect of them will the worker be able to make appropriate referrals to other agencies: only

then will he be able to show the client why such a referral will be useful. Currently about half the people referred to specialist services fail to reach them (Ritson 1981); the likely explanation for this is that the clients have not understood why the referrals were being made, nor felt they could gain from taking them up.

2. Some referrals to the social worker will be clients who have already received help from a specialist agency such as an ATU. If the worker is to provide appropriate help for these clients he will need to know something of the approach the specialist agency takes, and what expectations of him it will have given clients. It will also be important for him to meet the clients in the company of key staff of the specialist agency so that together they can clarify priorities and provide continuity in the care offered.

3. Some people will be the clients of many agencies over a period of months or years and will be in touch with two or more at any particular time. Close collaboration between the staff of agencies will be necessary if such clients are to receive appropriate, consistent help.

4. New developments in service will be accomplished best in circumstances which encourage the exchange of ideas and a jointly agreed policy amongst the helping agents in the locality concerned.

Abstinence or controlled drinking?

The help offered to those with any medical or social problem must always be limited by the current level of knowledge about the problem and about the methods that can be employed to solve it. Knowledge about alcohol problems has not yet developed sufficiently to be certain which clients who have been over-using alcohol can safely return to moderate drinking. Consequently some agencies insist that total abstinence is the only proper goal for clients with alcohol problems, although others believe that for some clients the appropriate goal is moderate drinking. If the social worker is to understand the structure and orientation of available services, he needs a critical appreciation of this controversial issue.

In 1962, when lifelong abstinence was regarded as the only solution for people diagnosed 'alcoholic', Davies published a paper suggesting that some people treated for alcoholism do return to moderate drinking. This seemed to directly contradict the view, current at the time, that alcoholism is an illness for which no cure is known and that it remains latent in the individual whose condition has been arrested as a result of total abstinence. Any attempt at social drinking was thought to lead inevitably to continual, uncontrolled drinking. Although alcohol treatment units established abstinence as their primary goal in the following decade, some studies (e.g. Sobell and Sobell 1976) supported the idea that a return to moderate drinking may be possible.

During the same period the data showing the relationship between per capita consumption and alcohol problems (de Lint and Schmidt 1971) offered another challenge to the notion that alcoholism is an illness that can be contained (by abstinence) but not cured, as did evidence suggesting some people become abstinent or learn to drink moderately without help from any agency. (This phenomenon is misleadingly described as 'spontaneous remission' since the change in drinking behaviour is frequently associated with a change in life circumstances, such as getting married.)

Many questions were raised about the reliability of these data, but more recently an important large-scale study, funded by the Rand Corporation and carried out in America, has provided detailed follow-up data at six months, 18 months and four years (Armor *et al.* 1978; Polich *et al.* 1980; colloquially described as the Rand Reports). Its findings strongly support the views that:

1. over time a significant proportion of people who receive help with alcohol problems will have periods of abstinence or moderate drinking interspersed with one or more relapses into uncontrolled drinking;
2. those with a commitment to moderate drinking are almost as likely to remain free of alcohol problems (over a four-year period) as those with a long-term commitment to abstinence.

It now seems possible to draw two conclusions from the available evidence. Firstly, more careful matching of clients to the kind of help offered may decrease the frequency of periods of relapse into problem drinking. Secondly, some people can return to normal social drinking. However, it is quite clear that the goal of moderate drinking is not appropriate for all or even for the majority of people with alcohol problems.

Who, then, can safely be encouraged to attempt a return to moderate drinking? Unfortunately no definitive answer to this important question can be provided at present. However, it seems likely that moderate drinking may be the appropriate goal where the person refuses to consider abstinence; where there are strong external demands on the person to drink socially; where the person presents no physical signs of dependence and has an intact family; and where help oriented towards the goal of abstinence has already proved ineffective (Hodgson 1979; Polich *et al.* 1980). Hodgson also suggests that abstinence should be the appropriate goal where:

1. physical disorders (e.g. progressive liver disease) which could be exacerbated by drinking are present;
2. the person has recently suffered serious withdrawal symptoms;
3. uncontrolled or bizarre behaviour following moderate drinking is frequently demonstrated;
4. there is strong external pressure to become abstinent, or a personal commitment to abstinence;
5. the person is currently sustaining abstinence following a history of severe alcohol problems; or
6. previous help oriented to moderation has failed to facilitate a change in drinking behaviour.

Thus the more severely alcohol dependent clients seem the least likely to be able to sustain a moderate level of drinking (Edwards and Gross 1976; Polich *et al.* 1980). Furthermore, researchers and specialist practitioners in Britain and America are generally agreed that it is necessary for every individual in whom a serious drinking problem has been identified to become alcohol free and to remain abstinent for a time. This ensures that any withdrawal symptoms can be eliminated and that the person has time to develop a better understanding of the harm caused by over-use of alcohol. During the period of abstinence the person concerned and the agency staff in contact with him can hope to make a realistic appraisal of his ability to learn to drink moderately.

Specialist workers have sometimes been reluctant to establish any goal other than abstinence because the criteria for determining when controlled drinking is a possible long-term solution are imprecise (Glatt 1980). Some agencies, notably AA, dispute the evidence that controlled drinking is possible for some and continue to insist that lifelong abstinence is the only valid approach for anyone whose drinking has caused them or their family harm. This cautious approach is understandable: abstinence may seem the safe course to advise in uncertain circumstances. However, it is clearly not acceptable to all clients and its strong advocacy may cause some to reject all attempts to help. It may also be positively unhelpful to reinforce in clients the belief that loss of control is inevitable if they drink even a little, as they may grow to assume it is pointless to try to drink in moderation and abandon themselves to excessive, harmful quantities on every drinking occasion.

Clearly the social worker must be cautious about encouraging clients to try to drink moderately. The worker should keep in mind the importance of an alcohol free period during which withdrawal symptoms can be eliminated, appropriate medical examination completed and the extent of the alcohol problems explored. If these are to be realistic possibilities for clients, the social worker has to be in a position to arrange access to appropriate local medical and support services.

The available services

The introductory paragraphs of this chapter identify that services are needed to meet acute, urgent problems, to assess the nature of drinking problems and to enable the client to achieve sobriety, and to help with the longer term readjustment in relationships and lifestyle. The remainder of this chapter describes the ways in which the health service, residential and day care facilities and counselling and self-help groups currently help to meet these needs.

Health service provision

1. *Alcoholism treatment units* There are now about three dozen specialist treatment units in Britain. It is estimated that slightly more than a third of those with alcohol problems who are treated within the health service are patients in ATUs. Most are small, autonomously functioning units within psychiatric hospitals, but some are within the psychiatric departments of district general hospitals. Unit staff generally expect to provide a follow-up service: some units have close links with residential, day care and fieldwork services in the local community and some also have a community nurse attachment.

Most units have a planned programme of treatment which includes a range of group and individual activities. The usefulness of people who have similar problems working together to explore the problems and their solution through group discussion is emphasised, but individual counselling is also offered. Some units include programmes designed to teach moderate drinking, although only a proportion of patients are offered this alternative to total abstinence. Patients aiming to remain abstinent are sometimes encouraged to take Abstem or Antabuse. These substances block alcohol metabolism and, when taken before alcohol, produce nausea, headache and breathlessness. Some people are able to establish abstinence more easily when they know that they cannot safely drink on any day they have taken an Abstem tablet.

Individual counselling and groupwork may be based on cognitive, behavioural or psychodynamic approaches to helping, and may be the responsibility of psychiatrist, nurse, social worker, psychologist or occupational therapist. Many units have worked hard at developing multidisciplinary teamwork within the setting and try to make sure that every patient receives help from the team members who have the skills which will be most useful to them.

The units usually have an established procedure through which each referral is assessed and the capacity of the unit to help is estimated. Units often accept self-referrals and referrals from social work agencies, although it is usual to keep the relevant general practitioner informed about each person to whom any service is offered. Those units with in-patient beds try to complete the in-patient phase of help within two to six weeks. Because there is no substantial evidence to demonstrate that in-patient care improves the individual's chances of changing his drinking behaviour, a smaller proportion of referrals is offered admission than formerly. It is most often offered to those who are unlikely to be able to stop drinking and achieve a period of abstinence without considerable medical and nursing support and those for whom a period of relief from external stresses seems necessary.

Unit staff usually continue contact with each individual after the initial intensive period of treatment. Patients who participate in after-care are more likely to reduce or stop drinking, and although people differ in the extent to which they need further help, continued contact for the three to six month period which follows establishing abstinence or moderate drinking is generally associated with successful outcome. Those who are no longer members of intact families or who are homeless or unemployed seem to have greater need of a variety of follow-up facilities for a longer period of time. After-care may be carried out in collaboration with other community based services and may continue for a year or more.

The staff of some ATUs provide a consultancy service for general practitioners and social workers because they have come to recognise that 'generalist' primary care workers are able to provide help for a wide range of people with alcohol problems who might otherwise not have been assessed as needing help until their problems became very severe. It is also acknowledged that the support of 'specialists' may be important if primary care workers are to develop confidence and skill in working with problem drinkers.

2. *Psychiatry* Traditionally alcoholism has been regarded as a psychiatric illness and the medical practitioners who have been pioneers in this subject in Britain have usually been psychiatrists, so it can be expected that the general psychiatry services will be readily available to those ATU patients who need them and that in those health regions (health boards in Scotland) which have insufficient or no special treatment units, the general psychiatry service will offer help. In England and Wales 7 per cent of all admissions to general psychiatry services in 1975 had a diagnosis of alcoholism, that is 35.5 admissions per 100,000 of the population aged 15 years and over (Advisory Committee on Alcoholism 1978). It is generally held that treatment in a psychiatric unit is less successful than that in an ATU: certainly general psychiatry wards have contained few medical or nursing staff with knowledge about or interest in developing facilities to meet the particular treatment needs of people with alcohol related problems. This situation may be changing, as some area health authorities are now designating one consultant psychiatrist with special responsibility for developing and maintaining services for problem drinkers.

3. *Detoxification* Two groups of people with serious alcohol problems experience particular difficulties during the process of becoming alcohol free and require special help:

(a). some people who are alcohol dependent suffer severe withdrawal symptoms and *delirium tremens* when drinking is stopped. They need continual medical assistance for several days so that the worst excesses of this condition can be prevented or controlled;

(b). habitual and homeless drunken offenders have frequently found difficulty in securing referral to appropriate agencies and in making use of them when referred. It seems they are more likely to have their needs carefully assessed and to accept referral for appropriate longer term help from an agency especially designed to help them through the process of becoming alcohol free.

Although the basic components of care required to meet the specific needs of these two types of client are the same as those provided for others being helped to 'dry out', the emphasis will be different. It is, therefore, appropriate to provide detoxification facilities in a variety of settings.

During detoxification the person will often require medication to reduce the unpleasantness and severity of the physical and psychological symptoms of withdrawal (see Chapter 2) and to correct any serious nutritional deficiency. A careful medical examination will be needed to clarify whether specific alcohol related disabilities (such as peripheral neuritis, cirrhosis or injury sustained through falling when drunk) are present and require treatment. Other disorders, such as chest infection, which have become chronic through neglect, will be diagnosed and treatment for them initiated.

Detoxification is an unpleasant process and the person who has experienced serious withdrawal symptoms on earlier occasions is likely to be agitated and frightened. The support and reassuring presence of nursing, medical and social work staff, and, if detoxification takes place at home, of spouse or friends, is a crucial part of any service. After two to three days most people will be up and about and able to think more rationally about their situation.

It will often be possible for a person to 'dry out' at home, with the general practitioner and community nurse providing whatever medical and nursing assistance is necessary. The more severely alcohol dependent person may need continuous medical and nursing care and is more likely to require admission to hospital. ATUs offer help with detoxification to their patients, but other types of hospital unit regularly provide special facilities. In some localities, for example, a consultant physician in the gastro-intestinal unit of the district general hospital agrees to make a number of his beds available for people requiring detoxification: in other areas beds are made available in admission wards of psychiatric units.

It has long been recognised that habitual and homeless drunken offenders are not much helped by arrest and fine or imprisonment, and the Home Office Working Party Report on Habitual Drunken Offenders (1971) advocated that ways be found to divert them from the criminal justice system. The Criminal Justice Act of 1972 introduced a practical alternative to arrest (section 34). This made it possible for the police in England and Wales to take drunken offenders, who were willing, to a treatment centre which had been approved for this purpose by the Secretary of State for Health and Social Services, instead of arresting them. The Act made it clear that drunken offenders would be under no compulsion to stay at such a centre, although the centre staff might encourage them to do so. Two centres, intended as pilot projects, were approved in the late 1970s and the Department of Health and Social Security funded a major research project to examine the service they provided. Although the research shows that neither of the two centres has been thoroughly successful, it does support the argument that special facilities are needed for the habitual and homeless drunken offender. A variety of ways of developing such facilities is now emerging. In England and Wales it is proving possible for services designed to meet local needs to develop without the formal designation of detoxification centres, and the 'wet centres' recently proposed by the Home Secretary may provide another alternative to arrest. In Scotland, clause 5 of the Criminal Justice Act (Scotland) 1980 gives the police power to take habitual drunken offenders to 'designated places' as an alternative to arrest, thus making it possible to introduce them to helping agencies with special concern for their particular needs.

4. *General hospital facilities* Specialist services concerned with the physical disorders consequent upon alcohol over-use will be important to many clients. The alcohol related physical disorders described in Chapter 2 include conditions that are likely to require both surgical and medical intervention. Referral to gastroenterologists, cardiologists and neurologists may be required by those who misuse alcohol.

The accident and emergency service of each district general hospital provides an important resource for homeless alcoholics and habitual drunken offenders who injure themselves whilst drunk, for those who, whilst under the influence of alcohol, are involved in road accidents and for those who are found comatose either because of rapidly ingesting a very large quantity of alcohol or through drinking whilst taking sedative drugs such as barbiturates.

There is evidence to suggest that referrals to general hospital facilities are sometimes made without recognition of the relevance of alcohol use to the situation and that hospital staff are not always quick to establish the relationship between alcohol misuse and the condition they are treating. However, perhaps in part as a result of the work of the Medical Council on Alcholism, the significance of alcohol use in the causation of a number of serious disorders seems to be of increasing interest to medical researchers and practitioners. Social workers based in general hospitals may be of particular help in initiating assessment of the significance of alcohol as a cause of illness and, where appropriate, in arranging for specialist counselling facilities to be available.

5. *General practitioner services* Research studies (e.g. Wilkins 1974) show that people with alcohol problems consult their general practitioner significantly more often than the population at large, but that they seldom raise the question of their alcohol use with the general practitioner, and that general practitioners are not well informed about the consequences of alcohol over-use, so seldom initiate discussion about drinking behaviour with patients.

As a primary care agent, the general practitioner is clearly well placed to notice problems at a relatively early stage of development. The current trend towards community based services (Report of Advisory Committee 1978) gives emphasis to the significant part he may be able to play in both the identification and the continuing care of people with alcohol problems. It has been suggested that general practitioners can often provide all the necessary medical care and that, if they work in collaboration with social workers and community nurses, the needs of many people with alcohol problems can be met without referral to specialist facilities. Four advantages flow from such a community based approach:

1. the degree of disruption in the client's life can be reduced by avoiding hospital admission;
2. his family is immediately involved in the resolution of his alcohol problems;
3. the demand for expensive hospital facilities should be reduced; and
4. if general practitioners can be persuaded to develop greater skill in the identification of alcohol problems they will improve their ability to refer relevantly to the specialist medical services, and to identify the physical disorders associated with alcohol abuse at an earlier stage than usually occurs at present.

Homeless problem drinkers have a chronic need for medical care for a variety of disabling illnesses, such as bronchitis, and for accidental injury. Voluntary agencies specialising in work with the homeless have made particular efforts to interest general practitioners in the medical care of this group, and a handful (e.g. Pollak 1970) have carried out pioneering work which highlights the considerable need for medical provision for the homeless and the difficulties of providing it.

Residential facilities

The available residential provision includes both special facilities designed for people with alcohol problems and facilities provided for a broader category of clients (e.g. the single homeless) which is recognised as including a proportion who over-use alcohol. Over the last ten years, and especially since the DHSS circular of 1973, voluntary agencies in England and Wales have established a range of new residential facilities. A smaller number has recently developed in Scotland, where agencies may have been encouraged by a Social Work Services Group circular in 1976 and the availability of grants under section 10 of the Social Work (Scotland) Act 1968. The voluntary agencies concerned have often received support, including some finance, from local authority departments, but local authorities have seldom established their own facilities for clients who misuse alcohol. (Manchester Social Services Department, which established a hostel in the early 1970s and Lothian Social Work Department, which has taken responsibility for a hostel which was previously part of a time-limited voluntary agency project, provide examples of what local authorities might do.) Some voluntary agencies, like the Alcohol Recovery Project, have focused on the particular needs of people on 'skid row' and others, such as Turning Point, have established hostels and half-way houses for the broad range of people with alcohol related difficulties.

The existing residential facilities are of three types:

1. *Shelters and lodging houses* Although residential accommodation in government-run reception centres and commercial lodging houses has been decreasing in recent years, these facilities, together with the night shelters and houses run by agencies such as the Cyrenians and the Salvation Army, provide basic overnight shelter, food and warmth for those on 'skid row', for single homeless casual labourers and recently discharged prisoners and psychiatric patients who are drinking harmfully. Staff try to establish the kind of contact with clients that makes it possible to discuss the advisability of stopping drinking and attempting to develop a different way of life, but are often limited in the help they can give because of working conditions and poor staffing levels. In addition, as Archard (1979) has described in graphic detail, the circumstances of clients make breaking away from 'skid row' or the current drinking school a gargantuan feat.

2. *Hostels* Special hostel facilities have developed for those trying to move away from the 'skid row' way of life and for people for whom a period of residential care is a necessary half-way stage in the process of readjusting to a broken marriage, or work, or a

changed pattern of social activity. Some hostels provide an alternative to in-patient care in a hospital unit; others are designed for those who need continuing help after leaving hospital. In most hostels residents are expected to be totally abstinent; residents who drink are usually required to leave, although they may be re-admitted after demonstrating a renewed commitment to abstinence. A few hostels aim to enable people to learn to drink moderately and would not normally admit clients aiming to maintain total abstinence. The regimes within the houses vary widely, but there are two broad categories – those whose regimes provide a rehabilitation programme through which residents will pass, and those which have no formal programme and instead of emphasising rehabilitation, focus on sharing and friendship between staff and residents within the community which the hostel constitutes (Otto and Orford 1978; Archard 1979). Hostels vary in the extent to which they use groupwork and individual counselling methods.

Although there is no clear evidence that one type of hostel is more successful than another in helping people to change their life-style and their use of alcohol, hostel staff usually prefer to place 'skid row' people in separate establishments from other problem drinkers during the early stages of rehabilitation. As the 'skid row' people experience special difficulties in developing an alcohol-free life-style, it seems to be more helpful to bring them together in a hostel where these difficulties can be the focus of attention. In addition, people either recently discharged from an ATU or using a hostel as an alternative to in-patient care may not sufficiently established in their own sobriety to cope with the 'breakouts' to which those recently on 'skid row' seem prone.

Many hostels do not have resident staff as it is thought to be advantageous to provide an environment which encourages residents to learn by experience how to make satisfactory social and domestic arrangements. In some hostels it is argued that it is necessary to make available the additional support resident staff can offer. Residents, whether or not they have been living on 'skid row', often need to remain in a hostel for many months.

3. *Sheltered housing* Sheltered housing in small group homes and housing associations provides a necessary service for two groups of clients. It provides a permanent home for clients who continue to require a minimum level of support and assistance, and where it is an integral part of an agency providing hostel care, it offers a

further point on a pathway to independent living. When the individual demonstrates to himself the ability to cope well with minimum support, he will move into his own accommodation; in all probability this will signal his movement out of the sphere of helping agencies altogether.

Day care facilities

Some day care facilities are available at hospital treatment units, but here the focus is on services provided by social service agencies. The facilities include shop fronts, day time shelters, workshops and training centres. Shop fronts often provide the first point of contact with rehabilitation services for homeless problem drinkers. Agency staff aim to help callers into detoxification facilities, arrange general medical treatment and encourage callers to consider moving into a hostel where they can establish sobriety. Day time shelters may serve a similar function, but workshops are usually designed for those who, although they have already made a commitment to abstinence, are not yet able to cope with a job in the open market.

Some day time shelters and workshops provide a service for a wide range of clients, amongst whom will be included a proportion who have alcohol problems. These are similar to the day centres run in some probation and after care departments. The Criminal Justice Act (1972) made provision (section 20) for some offenders placed on probation to be required to attend a day training centre for not more than 60 days. This provision is aimed at the 'inadequate recidivist whose offences reflect a lack of basic social skill' (Home Office 1972). The centres may offer remedial education, work training, matrimonial counselling and home economics. Four probation areas were designated to establish pilot projects - Glamorgan, Inner London, Liverpool and Sheffield: other probation departments provide day care for recidivists on probation and for recently discharged prisoners. A proportion of people attending these centres have alcohol problems, and in some instances special attention is given to their particular needs.

Local authorities have not been quick to establish day centres and sheltered workshops, although those that exist for the mentally ill sometimes offer provision to people with alcohol problems. Few agencies seem to have developed opportunities for job experience for clients recovering from alcohol problems.

Counselling and self-help agencies

Two agencies – Alcoholics Anonymous and the National Council on Alcoholism (in Scotland, the Scottish Council on Alcoholism) – have developed during the last 30 years to become important sources of help to a significant number of people with alcohol problems. The National Council (NCA) and the Scottish Council (SCA) have facilitated the establishment of local councils which provide information services and personal counselling, and AA has developed a network of support groups throughout the country. Both types of agency actively involve people who have direct personal experience of alcohol problems in organising and providing services. AA is an organisation for alcoholics run entirely by alcoholics; the councils on alcoholism draw on the skills and knowledge of specialist helping agents, of people who have resolved their own alcohol related problems and of other local volunteers.

1. *Counselling services* The NCA was founded in 1962, and the first local council began in Liverpool in 1963. Since that time councils have developed in urban and rural areas in many parts of Britain, and in 1980 there were 34 councils in England and Wales and 18 in Scotland. The first councils were information centres disseminating basic facts to the general public, to welfare agencies and to industrial and commercial companies.

The counselling services of the local councils developed to some extent as a consequence of their success in improving public understanding of alcohol over-use. People appreciated that their drinking, or their spouses' drinking, may be at the root of their difficulties and called at councils to ask how to contact specialist services, or simply to express their distress to someone who might be able to provide support and reassurance. The directors of councils, whether they were recovered alcoholics, or nurses, or social workers were able to offer appropriate counselling. However, as the number of callers increased it became clear that additional counsellors, who could also provide a high quality of service, would have to be recruited.

During the last five years local councils have recruited considerable numbers of volunteer counsellors and have developed part-time training programmes for them. These programmes focus on understanding the nature and range of alcohol problems and the services available to clients, and on learning the basic skills of counselling. Once they have successfully completed the training, counsellors begin working with clients under the supervision of a more skilled and experienced person. Local psychiatrists, social workers and other concerned professionals also offer consultation. Little use of groupwork seems to be made by counsellors, but a variety of individual counselling methods are used. Some clients are offered a programme designed to help them learn to reduce their alcohol use to a non-harmful level, but for many clients the appropriate goal of counselling is thought to be abstinence.

The services of councils are freely available to whoever calls at the office or telephones. Councils may provide help for spouses whose partners refuse to acknowledge the significance of their alcohol problems, but the bulk of work is with people who are currently over-using alcohol. The clientele includes some 18–25 year olds who would be unlikely to seek help from medical agencies, and some councils are providing counselling services for individual companies which have recognised that alcohol problems are significantly affecting the work performance of employees.

The local councils on alcoholism continue to expand their counselling services, and as individual councils build a corps of trained and experienced counsellors, an important specialist service may emerge. Such a service could become a helpful complement to that available from local authorities and probation departments.

2. *Alcoholics Anonymous* AA is the best known and perhaps the most readily available of the agencies which help people with alcohol problems. The organisation was formed in the USA in the 1930s, and the first British group was established in London in 1948. It rapidly expanded in the 1950s and 1960s, and by 1978 there were over 1,000 groups in Britain.

Members come from many different social and cultural circumstances. They are predominantly middle-aged (average age of joining seems to remain around 40), but not inevitably middle class. Although in earlier days a tiny minority of members were women, by 1978 women constituted a third of the membership. Unlike the local councils on alcoholism, AA does not attract many people at an early stage in the development of alcohol problems. In his study of AA in England and Wales, Robinson (1979) states that 'AA is still for most people, a last hope organisation' (p. 28) and that many members have experienced severe symptoms of alcohol dependence.

The AA programme of recovery is dependent for its success on the individual accepting himself as 'alcoholic'. For AA this acceptance involves understanding 'his basic "being" as alcoholic rather than as normal and non-alcoholic'. The AA member *is* an alcoholic rather than a person who *has* alcoholism (Robinson p. 59). The organisation shows little interest in causation and is convinced it is impossible for an alcoholic to learn to drink moderately. The alcoholic is described as having a physical allergy to drink, so 'one drink means one drunk'. He is also perceived as having an 'alcoholic personality' which is defined as immature and self-centred: he is thought to be spiritually sick and is not expected to recover until he has accepted the existence of a 'higher power' than himself. The basis of the AA approach is a set of beliefs for which research has so far produced no supporting evidence. However, AA is remarkably successful in helping some people with severe alcohol problems.

The two central components to the help offered are the AA group meeting, and the fellowship offered through informal contact between members. The local AA group is the means through which information about alcohol problems and the recovery programme are disseminated. At open meetings non-members, including interested professional workers, are welcomed: closed meetings, attended only by AA members, focus on issues it is felt only acknowledged alcoholics can properly understand. Every member of AA is entitled to attend the meetings of other groups, and many members regularly attend more than one group. There is considerable variation in the groups. Some concentrate on the problems of becoming and remaining abstinent, whilst others are more concerned with long-term issues (not directly related to drinking) which impose stress on the individual and consequently may produce in him the attitudes and behaviours associated with his previous drinking lifestyle. Because groups are so varied new members are encouraged to visit several before deciding which to join.

Each new member is introduced to 'The Twelve Steps' which are offered as a guide to a new abstinent lifestyle.

The Twelve Steps

1. Admitted we were powerless over alcohol – that our lives had become unmanageable.
2. Came to believe that a Power greater than ourselves could restore us to sanity.

3. Made a decision to turn our will and our lives over to the care of God as we understood Him.
4. Made a searching and fearless moral inventory of ourselves.
5. Admitted to God, to ourselves and to another human being the exact nature of our wrongs.
6. Were entirely ready to have God remove all these defects of character.
7. Humbly asked Him to remove our shortcomings.
8. Made a list of all persons we had harmed, and became willing to make amends to them all.
9. Made direct amends to such people wherever possible, except when to do so would injure them or others.
10. Continued to take personal inventory and when we were wrong, promptly admitted it.
11. Sought through prayer and meditation to improve our conscious contact with God as we understood Him praying only for knowledge of His will for us and the power to carry that out.
12. Having had a spiritual awakening as the result of these steps, tried to carry this message to alcoholics and to practice these principles in all our affairs.

It is emphasised that an individual does not have to commit himself to all of the steps and AA literature acknowledges that some people may find some of the precepts unacceptable. AA denies that it is a religious organisation although it acknowledges The Twelve Steps are based on spiritual values. The alcoholic is described as behaving as if alcohol is the power greater than himself: all that is necessary is that alcohol is replaced by another power which may be God, but could as well be the AA group, for through membership of the group it is possible to achieve what could not be achieved alone (i.e. abstinence).

Talking is the basic activity of the AA group. At each meeting there is formally organised talk, during which a number of people may 'tell their story'. This story is usually concerned with the past and with drinking behaviour but it may be about current issues that are producing anxiety and causing recovery to be impeded. Membership is not dependent on being able to 'tell your story', but it seems that more than three-quarters of members have done so at some time. Informal activity is an important component of every meeting. An established member will introduce himself to a newcomer, looking for ways of introducing the principles of AA (and thereby, incidentally, providing himself the opportunity of pursuing the twelth step). This initial contact may then become the new member's sponsor, who will provide personal support and help in the early days of sobriety. Sponsors demonstrate their compassion and friendship by being available to give help at any time of the day or night.

AA members meet regularly for a variety of social activities. They visit each other's homes and are free to call on each other for help to cope with any stress or difficulty they may encounter. It is thought that offering help to others is as important in meeting the needs and sustaining the sobriety of the helper as it is of the helped. AA recognises that professionals such as psychiatrists, psychologists and social workers may offer special assistance, but sees the help alcoholics are able to provide for each other as the crucial element (Alibrandi 1978).

Some members grow away from AA as they become securely established in their abstinence. For others it becomes a way of life: their ties with former friends weaken and they develop a friendship network within AA. On average people remain in membership for about five years, and although many members drop in and out of the fellowship, many remain for ten years or longer. AA willingly offers a service in prisons and hospitals and tries to ensure its fellowship is constantly available to any person who acknowledges his alcoholism and a wish to become abstinent.

3. *Al-Anon and Alateen* Al-Anon, an organisation for the relatives and friends of those who misuse alcohol, and its linked organisation Alateen for the children (aged 12–20) of alcoholics, are both based on The Twelve Steps of AA. They aim to provide comfort to the families of alcoholics, to enable family members to understand and give appropriate support to their alcoholic relatives and to provide opportunities for spiritual growth through adherence to The Twelve Steps. Like AA, these organisations hold to the view that alcoholism is a disease beyond the control of the sufferer. They recognise that alcohol problems are family problems and try to show that recrimination is unhelpful and that if patience, encouragement and a willingness to examine one's faults are demonstrated, the alcoholic will be helped to change his behaviour. The organisations make information about alcohol problems available to members and try to encourage a realistic approach to the difficulties of resolving them. About half the members are related to people who are active in AA, but the rest live with relatives who are still misusing alcohol.

5 Direct Work with the Identified Client

Sometimes, not only in his sleep,
He dreams about that other world, returns
To shiver in a grey chemise of sweat.

from *Reformed Drunkard* by Vernon Scannell

Books about the practice of social work usually describe it as purposeful, consciously thought out activity designed to enable the resolution of social problems and to facilitate personal growth. Writers emphasise that social work is about change and that the practitioner draws on specific knowledge, skills and values in his work with a client and the significant others in that client's family and social network. These notions form the basis of this chapter and of Chapter 6. This orientation to practice places emphasis on assessment as a continual process, on the careful planning and management of interventions and on determining priorities in individual cases and in the overall work load.

Clients with alcohol related problems have an obvious need to achieve change in their drinking patterns. If this change is to be maintained it is likely other changes will also be necessary. The life-style and attitudes of the identified client may become a focus for change (e.g. he may wish to develop new interests or to learn how to refuse a drink when it is offered); the behaviour and attitude of spouse and family may become a legitimate focus for change (e.g. a husband may need to readjust his behaviour and expectations once his wife achieves sobriety and demonstrates competence and interest in a range of activities) or a change may be necessary in the approach of an employer and workmates (e.g. when someone who has previously been carried by colleagues at work and whose opinion could be ignored, emerges in sobriety as a strong-minded person with ideas).

The application of systems theory in social work has helped practitioners appreciate the importance at initial assessment of both the proper identification of the client's core problem and of the elements (systems) within the client's network that will require change if that problem is to be satisfactorily resolved. The account of Mrs Charmond's situation (Chapter 3) makes clear the necessity for change in her relationships at work and within her social network, as well as in her drinking pattern. It is probable that all these changes can be accomplished through focus on change in Mrs Charmond – in her drinking, in her attitude and approach at work and in her skills in developing a range of satisfying interests and relationships. Mr Coney's situation provides an example of the use of systems analysis to identify the ways in which a change in behaviour in the client impacts on the systems of which he is a member and to clarify what interventions may be needed.

> Mr Coney, a docker of 57, had cirrhosis of the liver and oesophageal varices when he accepted that he had a serious alcohol problem and should become and remain abstinent. Both Mr Coney and his wife understood that he was likely to die if he continued drinking. Maintaining abstinence was crucial, but difficult because of the structure of Mr Coney's social network. The system within which he worked was one in which regular heavy drinking was common and the expectation that he would drink regularly was particularly great within Mr Coney's work group. These dockers were employed full time in the loading of cement powder: an extremely dusty and heavy job, made slightly more bearable because they spent lunch time slaking their thirst with several pints of beer and made a visit to the Dockers' Club for another drink as soon as work finished. The difficulty for Mr Coney of insisting on drinking only non-alcoholic beverages in the company of his work mates was great. A second difficulty was that the social melieu to which Mr Coney belonged was one in which manliness was strongly associated with drinking – with evenings spent in bars to which few women came and coach outings with all-male groups in which part of the day was taken up with drinking. Mr Coney was regarded as a fun loving, gregarious, good companion and valued the position in the neighbourhood this perception gave him. When assessing Mr Coney's need for help after discharge from an ATU, the social worker concluded that he would not be able to maintain abstinence unless some members of his friendship group understood its importance, accepted he could remain an enjoyable companion even although he did not drink, and supported his decision to abstain in the face of pressure from other friends. Thirdly, Mr Coney's family system was not geared to provide the support and encouragement he needed to maintain his abstinence. Although Mrs Coney accepted the importance of her husband remaining abstinent she was not prepared for the other

changes which that precipitated. The family home was her domain and she did not expect Mr Coney to spend much of his spare time there. Her position was challenged when he began to stay at home in the evenings and to take an interest in how she spent her time. Mrs Coney's social network consisted of her sisters, her married daughters and their children and women neighbours, and her pattern of activities was disrupted by, what seemed to her, too-frequent suggestions by Mr Coney that the two of them go out together in the evening and that he join her Saturday shopping expeditions.

Mr Coney's two daughters and their husbands, and his 19 year old son all found the changes he had made in his pattern of living disturbing. None of them fully understood the seriousness of his condition, nor that alcohol over-use was its cause; they thought his behaviour strange as well as irritating. It was clear that the members of his family could unwittingly undermine Mr Coney's decision to remain abstinent unless some readjustment in roles and relationships could be accomplished.

The social worker judged that intervention was needed within both the family system and the friendship group, and that she and Mr Coney would need to consider (in conjunction with the hospital staff who were providing follow-up services) what means he could devise for coping with and reducing the pressure to drink with his workmates. Systems theory helped the worker in this example to identify the targets for change. It also helped to clarify that normative behaviour (e.g. heavy weekend drinking at the Dockers' Club and highly differentiated roles between marriage partners – (see Bott 1957) may damage members of a socio-cultural group, and that it may be legitimate to intervene to modify the way in which norms are applied to particular individuals.

Once the systems analysis is complete the social worker can re-evaluate the factors which influence the client's capacity and motivation for change (see pp. 35–6, Chapter 3) and identify the order of priority of work with the client and his family and social network. It may be necessary to be involved concurrently with the identified client and with significant others, or it may be more appropriate to tackle issues sequentially. For example, it seemed necessary to work with Mr Coney and his wife concurrently. Mr Coney urgently needed skills that would help him sustain his decision to be abstinent, and active support from the people of most significance to him. As one of the psychiatrists in the hospital unit was continuing contact with Mr Coney through his weekly out-patient group, it was also necessary to clarify whether or not the social worker should confine herself to working with Mrs Coney and the family. After discussion between Mr Coney, the social worker and the psychiatrist, it was agreed that Mr Coney's immediate concerns at work would be addressed in the group (with the possibility of joint discussion between the psychiatrist, social worker and Mr Coney when this seemed appropriate) whilst the social worker explored issues with Mrs Coney and other members of the family. Work within the wider social network followed when some success had been achieved in the first two areas.

The initial focus of work in Mr Clare's case was rather different.

> Mr Clare was a schoolteacher whose current employment and future career were in jeopardy. Although he had recently gained control of his drinking and was demonstrating some ability in his work, his head teacher and the local education authority thought his earlier erratic behaviour and over-use of alcohol were evidence of unsuitability for the work. Mrs Clare was distressed and angry about her husband's drinking, but demonstrated concern and support once he accepted excessive drinking lay at the centre of his difficulties. It was concluded that the most urgent need was the resolution of Mr Clare's problems at work; only when these were resolved did the social worker engage with Mr and Mrs Clare in exploration of residual difficulties within their marriage.

Clearly the ordering of interventions by the social worker will be determined by the unique circumstances of each client.

The remainder of this chapter focuses on direct work with people who have been misusing alcohol; Chapter 6 discusses work with members of the family and social network.

Group and individual settings for social work intervention

A tradition has grown up in agencies concerned with people with alcohol related problems that their clients are more effectively helped in group settings. AA gives emphasis to the powerfulness of the group, ATUs generally include a variety of therapeutic groups in their programmes, and many specialist hostels regard group activities and the weekly group meeting as the principle means through which help is given. In addition, a number of the techniques and methods which seem particularly useful in the resolution of the problems clients bring are best used within a group. Social skills training, methods derived from Gestalt therapy, transactional analysis and other schools of dynamic psychotherapy are all ways of intervening that are designed for use in a small group (5–12) meeting regularly over a period of weeks or months. And behavioural methods which enable clients to learn to drink moderately frequently follow initial individual work with group activities designed to support, review and develop change in drinking behaviour.

A number of factors are presented to support the view that help within a group of people who have alcohol problems may be particularly effective.

1. Clients value the support and concern of others who have personal experience of the problems that result from alcohol over-use. They frequently express the view that other group members 'really know what it is like' and this sense of identification with each other facilitates the development of trust and openness. The special significance attached to identification with a group of peers by adolescents and young adults increases the potential of the small group setting for helping young people who have alcohol problems.
2. The special understanding of alcohol problems group members bring enables them to challenge unrealistic expectations or inappropriately defensive behaviour more effectively than the social worker. For example, the person who asserts that there is no harm in having a good drink on a Friday night will be reminded of the frequent occasions on which his Friday spree has caused problems at home and at work, and the person who describes his children as difficult and unresponsive will be asked to think about the effect on them of his drunken behaviour (Kessel and Walton pp. 137–8).
3. Group members will be particularly sensitive to pressures which may trigger a return to inappropriate drinking and will facilitate exploration of those pressures and of alternative responses to them.
4. Awareness that alcohol has been a cause of problems will be held by all group members and they will reinforce for each other the advantages of 'staying sober'.
5. Participants recognise each others' capacities and qualities and consequently enable the development of a better sense of worth and a perception of misuse of alcohol as a problem to be tackled rather than as a sign of degeneracy.

6. The success a group member demonstrates in changing his attitudes and behaviour serves to encourage others in their attempts to make changes.
7. The exploration of similar problems in other group members helps the individual to understand his own situation and to work out solutions to his difficulties.

This reasoning parallels that presented for groupwork with other types of client (e.g. Hartford 1972; Davies 1975; Douglas 1978). Perhaps the only surprise is that groups generally seem most helpful when they are composed entirely of people who have been misusing alcohol, even although the groups' attention will focus on getting and keeping a job, resolving marital and family difficulties, developing new interests and relationships and other concerns common to a wide range of clients for whom groupwork may be appropriate. The other group members' understanding of alcohol problems is particularly important in the early stages of sobriety when clients have specific concerns directly associated with alcohol use (e.g. coping with the desire to drink or with a slip back into uncontrolled drinking) which can be explored most easily in a group where they are of direct relevance to all members. It should also be remembered that the stigma which attaches to people with alcohol problems increases the likelihood of scapegoating and rejection within a group in which the problems of other members are unrelated to drink. It also helps to explain the value clients place on being with a group of other people who have the special understanding that personal experience of alcohol problems brings.

It has been suggested (Zimberg 1978) that the general advice that groups should be composed of people with alcohol problems does not apply to elderly people. It is thought that alcohol misuse in the elderly is frequently a response to social and psychological stresses associated with ageing, so the elderly person who develops an alcohol problem can be helped best through membership of a supportive and problem-solving group whose members are elderly and concerned with a range of problems of old age.

Although for many clients help in a group setting will be appropriate, it should be recognised that for some clients and for some problems a group is not a helpful setting. Women with alcohol problems often seem to need help based on an individual relationship at first and are only helped in a group once their sobriety is established and they have had an opportunity to develop a positive sense of identity. Three factors help to explain this. First, alcohol misuse in women is frequently a maladaptive response to a personal crisis (e.g. death of husband) rather than the end point of a long process of escalation from social to excessive drinking; if issues arising from the crisis are the essential early focus of intervention they are likely to be most easily resolved within a person-to-person relationship. Secondly, the stigma attached to alcohol abuse is greater for women than for men, and reinforces the woman client's feelings of despair and disgust about herself. This is an especial problem for women of 50 years or more whose drinking problems are of recent origin. Such clients are likely to need special reassurance and support in their efforts to overcome their guilt and shame and may find a group setting particularly threatening. Thirdly, the position of women in society is still such that many have low self-esteem and little experience of active involvement in open discussion or in activities in which they are on an equal footing with men.

It has been suggested that women are best helped in the later stages of intervention within a group composed entirely of women with alcohol problems. However, it is likely that a mixed group offers greater potential for the exploration and resolution of the problems many women have in their social and family relationships. In such a group it becomes possible to introduce a wide range of perspectives on an issue and to use methods, such as role-play, as a means through which group members can be provided with direct learning experiences about the impact they have on other people and about different ways of relating to others. Groupwork may be less useful for the surprisingly high proportion of women whose spouses also have alcohol problems: conjoint work (see Chapter 6) may be a more appropriate way of helping them.

The isolated individual, the person who has not yet been able to control his drinking and the person with practical or financial difficulties will all require individual help either as an alternative to group involvement or in addition to it. The example of Mr Whittle illustrates the importance of recognising when individual contact is more effective than group work.

> Mr Whittle, a widower of 46, lived alone in poor housing in an inner city area and had become isolated from his extended family and friends. His teenage sons were in residential care, one in a community for the profoundly handicapped over 100 miles distant, the other in a local children's home he was keen to leave in order to return to life in his home neighbourhood. Mr Whittle

was dominated by his isolation, his sense of guilt at his behaviour and his anger at the awful blows life had dealt him. He tried hard to maintain sobriety, but during the two years he had been in contact with the social worker he had been unable to manage this for longer than six weeks. Mr Whittle twice joined a group of clients with alcohol problems, but withdrew after a short time because his drunken behaviour and unkempt appearance prompted anger in other group members struggling hard to break away from old patterns. After he left the second group the worker arranged regular individual contact with Mr Whittle. In this setting it proved possible to continue working on becoming and remaining abstinent and to facilitate some contact between Mr Whittle and his sons that was enjoyable both for him and for them.

The use of different methods of intervention

Choosing the appropriate method of intervention may seem difficult in the current situation of uncertainty in social work about what is helpful and effective. The following points should help to increase clarity and the ability to act appropriately.

1. As clients with alcohol problems are a heterogeneous category, it is most unlikely that one method of social work will be equally suitable for all. For a method to be at all useful, however, it must facilitate work on the three fundamental concerns common to clients with alcohol problems, that is: achieving control of alcohol use (whether through abstinence or reduced intake) as quickly as possible; developing new sources of satisfaction; and enhancing capacity to handle stress without resort to uncontrolled drinking or other destructive behaviour.

2. In recent years there has been more emphasis on short-term work. This shift seems to be supported by the results of research studies (e.g. Orford and Edwards 1978) which indicate that brief intensive intervention is sufficient for some clients. However, there are two groups of client who seem to require very long-term help:

(a) those who have been living on 'skid row' for some time and who need several months of help before their abstinence is sufficiently well established for them to be able to begin building a new social network and establishing longer term aims for themselves;

(b) those for whom an abstinent life offers few satisfactions. These clients may have begun drinking heavily as a means of coping with long-standing personal problems which emerge with renewed vigour in spite of having stopped drinking, having a job and a comfortable home. They may appreciate the advantages of sobriety, yet be acutely unhappy and may return for help after many months of apparently managing well. Amongst this group are some who attempt, and succeed in committing, suicide.

3. Social workers, like other specialists, often give insufficient attention to the degree of congruence between the goals for a particular client and the methods of intervention used. Glaser *et al.* (1978) suggest that the consistency of success:failure ratios demonstrated by research studies is not an indicator that all methods of intervention are equally helpful (or unhelpful) but is a consequence of the failure to skilfully match method and client need. The implication is that careful matching will increase the social worker's ability to choose the approach which will be most effective in a particular situation. For example, although the question of whether clients aiming at controlled drinking and others committing themselves to the goal of abstinence can usefully work together in the same group has not been fully tested, it seems clear that at least some of those trying to sustain abstinence will be confused and upset by the presence in their group of others who are being encouraged to continue drinking - albeit at very much reduced levels - and that the different goals may be achieved best through different approaches to groupwork.

From the wide range of methods of intervention available to social workers three which seem particularly appropriately matched with problems commonly occurring as consequences of alcohol abuse have been selected for discussion here.

The problem-solving approach

By the time the assessment process is complete the worker and client will have established the areas in which change seems necessary and a tentative ordering of priorities. The worker will also have considered which methods of intervention seem likely to be most effective in achieving change in the areas to be tackled first. So, for example, in the case of Mrs Charmond (in Chapter 3) the worker not only identified with the client an order for the way in which they could proceed, but also indicated that he thought the problem-solving approach (Perlman 1957) to achieving change was appropriate. This particular method of intervention has specific advantages in direct individual work with clients with alcohol problems.

The method focuses on the current problems the client is experiencing. Although the process of assessment may result in some redefinition of their nature (e.g. Mrs Charmond brought problems of sleeplessness caused, she thought, by her nerves but the process of assessment introduced beverage alcohol as a cause) the problems defined by the client remain the central concern. The problem-solving approach recognises the importance of taking account of the 'whole person' but does not regard it as appropriate or necessary to attempt to explore and change the whole personality. Its primary goal is 'to help a person cope as effectively as possible with such problems in carrying social tasks and relationships which he now perceives, feels as stressful and finds insuperable without outside help' (Perlman 1970, p. 139). This approach may be particularly helpful to the alcohol dependent client full of remorse and preoccupied with 'how I came to be like this'. As Petty (1975) has indicated, treating alcohol dependence as a symptom of underlying psychopathology can so shift attention to uncovering the underlying cause that 'both alcoholic and helper become engaged in a long and fruitless search for the arsonist in the situation while the fire itself continues to rage'. Petty suggests that a preoccupation with causation may lead both the worker and the client to believe that drinking cannot be brought under control before the 'cause' is discovered. If the consequence of this belief is that no real attempt is made to reduce alcohol intake, the client is at serious risk of becoming increasingly physically damaged and increasingly hard to help through social work and medical interventions. The problem-solving approach not only avoids this risk, but has the positive advantage of giving serious attention to the problems brought by the client and of optimising his motivation and capacity to work on their resolution. Motivation and capacity are encouraged by two other aspects of the problem-solving approach which have particular relevance here.

The approach requires the formulation of realistic, achievable goals through the identification of quite specific difficulties, and thus allows the client to break down what may appear to be an overwhelmingly large problem into more manageable, more precisely defined concerns that are amenable to change. This process may itself serve to encourage the client into greater hope that action to improve things is possible and, thus, to increase his willingness to engage actively with the social worker in making changes in his situation. This will be particularly helpful for clients suffering the acute sense of hopelessness commonly associated with severe alcohol problems.

Because it focuses on realistic goals and encourages the client to draw on his own skills and capacities in achieving them, the problem-solving method is also helpful in increasing the possibility of some early experience of success for the client. In this way the development of his sense of worth is assisted, as is his confidence in his own abilities to cope with future problems. Involvement in establishing achievable goals, encouraging the client's participation in their achievement and facilitating some early experience of success is also likely to help increase the social worker's optimism and confidence about being able to intervene helpfully.

Mrs Charmond provided an example of the use of problem solving at the initial stages of contact. Miss Bridehead was able to make use of this approach at a later stage in the helping process, when a relationship with a concerned and supportive person was particularly important to her.

> Miss Bridehead, aged 28 years, moved to a hostel community for 12 people on discharge from in-patient care in an ATU. She had been abstinent for ten weeks and felt no compulsion to drink. She was unemployed, separated from family and friends and seriously lacking self-confidence. She felt miserable at her early failure at school and her inability to find satisfying work; she saw herself as a failure in her personal relationships, having accepted hospital admission at the point when an unhappy cohabitation finally broke down. Her friendships had always been with people she met in pubs and clubs, who drank regularly and in large quantities.

Although Miss Bridehead felt her past experience was a millstone she carried with her, she showed energy and courage in her wish to make her future more enjoyable, and in a vivid way demonstrated Perlman's concept of a 'person in process'. That is someone who is a product of his past, yet who is also involved in a process of becoming more (or less) than he was (Perlman 1970).

> Miss Bridehead identified two problems that she wanted to tackle – her unemployment and her difficulty in making new friends. She met weekly with her social worker to work on the unemployment issue, and through exploration of the problem, the kinds of satisfactions Miss Bridehead was looking for in a

job were established. With help from the worker in identifying career guidance resources Miss Bridehead began to search out information about particular types of work, and within six weeks gained employment as a van driver for a delivery service. She enjoyed the autonomy of this job and showed herself to be reliable and efficient.

Miss Bridehead used her contact with the social worker to discuss her anxieties (particularly her fear of responding to stress by drinking), as a support and reassurance in her efforts to sort out what she wanted for herself and as someone with whom she could share the satisfaction of finding a solution to her problem. The social worker demonstrated a number of the characteristics of the problem-solving approach as it is described by Perlman. She provided an accepting and encouraging relationship with Miss Bridehead and at the initial contact made sure that the worker and client established agreement about the problem to be tackled. By breaking the issue of unemployment into its component parts the worker was able to agree with Miss Bridehead the means of working towards problem resolution. Throughout, the client's capacity to discover things for herself was encouraged by the worker, so that she began to recognise her own abilities and effectiveness in solving the difficulties she had been experiencing and to develop greater self-esteem.

The description of social work practice using the problem-solving approach indicates that this method of work draws some of its characteristics from learning theory. The process of clarifying the problem and reducing it to its components obviously owes something to this theory, as does the focus on establishing realistic goals and the structuring of the intervention to reinforce the client's efforts to change his behaviour. Perlman readily acknowledges her debt to this theory and to the concepts developed in systems theory and crisis intervention.

The social skills approach

The mode of work chosen for dealing with Miss Bridehead's difficulty in making friends also owes a debt to learning theory and to the ideas developed in sensitivity training, organisational development and Gestalt therapy. This model of intervention is subsumed under the umbrella term social skills training. A recent book (Priestley *et al.* 1978) outlining this approach emphasises that personal change and the solving of problems is dependent on the ability to *learn* new ways of thinking and behaving. Although the authors describe their approach as entirely pragmatic, a set of concepts underpin the method and the process of helping is characterised by carefully thought out programmes, employing very particular techniques. The social worker using this approach has to be willing to give time and attention to the careful preparation of the work he is proposing for each programme. Social skills training is based on the notion that each problem presented by a client has three components: one concerned with information (e.g. about alcohol); the second concerned with attitude (e.g. to drinking and driving); and the third with practical skill (e.g. in sustaining a decision to be abstinent). The client's solution to his problem is perceived as dependent on his ability to take in new knowledge (e.g. about the physical effects of alcohol on the mind and body), to understand the feelings he attaches to the problem (e.g. about wanting to be 'one of the boys') and to develop practical ability in specific activities (e.g. in refusing to drink without causing offence). The worker devises a programme, in collaboration with his client, which provides learning opportunities in each of these three dimensions of the problem and its solution. Satisfactory programme construction requires clarification of the programme's aims, identification of realistic appropriate personal objectives by the client and the ability of the worker to draw on whatever range of written material, people, facilities and equipment are necessary to stimulate and assist the learning/change process in the client. The programme is usually designed for a group of clients with similar problems so that opportunities for sharing and comparing and a supportive environment within which clients can try out new ideas and behaviours can be provided. The presence of the group also makes possible the use of the wide range of available group activities and exercises.

In Miss Bridehead's case the group of 12 residents at the hostel met once each week with a residential social worker as group leader. This formally agreed commitment was understood to provide the opportunity to explore specific problems and to identify ways of solving them. It was expected that group members would try out their preferred solutions in the interval between meetings.

When Miss Bridehead identified the problem on which she wished to work it emerged that other group members also had difficulty establishing friendships. The group leader suggested they write on a sheet of paper, large enough for everyone to see, all the factors that helped to explain their current difficulty. The list was completed in ten minutes. It included common items like 'shyness' and 'I don't know what to say', direct indicators of low esteem such as 'other people are not much interested in me' and 'I've only ever had the courage to chat up a woman when I was drunk' and comments emerging from serious reflection such as 'I'm afraid I won't know when it's time to end a conversation' and 'How can you tell when it's all right to offer more than acquaintance?' The worker made no attempt to edit or comment on the list as it emerged, but when it was complete, worked with the group members at placing the items in categories. This done, it became possible to suggest group exercises that encouraged members to examine their behaviour and feelings in relation to each category of difficulty. The hour and a half session ended with members working in twos and threes on a specific aspect of the way they related to people that they would like to change.

Commitments were made to practise new ways of relating to others in the course of the following week: these 'experiments' were the first item for discussion at the following meeting, which went on to explore other components of the issue. The group used a variety of means for learning about how to enjoy familiar social situations, to join a new group of people with a common interest, and to offer hospitality. The leader introduced exercises which focused on risk taking, collaboration between individuals, and understanding another's feelings, as well as role-play of specific social situations. Material describing many local interest groups and societies was made available to group members, and they were supported in experimenting with outings they wanted to make to local cinemas, cafés, church activities, and so on.

It is readily apparent that once a problem is analysed the programme that is worked out for addressing it will be detailed, and that the worker will have to be careful in the use of time. It is easy to attempt too much in one session, especially in the early meetings of a group whose members have no previous knowledge of each other. The group of which Miss Bridehead was a member spent most of four meetings working on this one topic and returned to aspects of it at later meetings. The commitment to practise what has been learnt is important, and is reinforced by giving time at the following meeting to the discussion of 'homework'. This also enables any residual or newly identified difficulty to emerge and become the focus of further learning/change.

Miss Bridehead had the advantage of working within the group of people with whom she was currently living. This made it easy for her to find support in her efforts to experiment and change. However, the social skills approach can also be used by groups of clients who see each other only once a week.

> Mr South, a journalist aged 34 years, had been diagnosed alcoholic and admitted to a psychiatric hospital for 'drying out' on two occasions. His job seemed to require him to spend a good deal of time talking to people in public houses. He enjoyed his work, but wanted to learn how to say 'no' when he was offered a drink and to buy alcoholic drink for others and a soft drink for himself.

Mr South joined a group which met once each week with a social worker employed by a voluntary agency at a day care unit for problem drinkers and their families. The group included five others who were frequently placed in situations where they had difficulty abstaining from alcohol.

Timothy Tangs was a 19 year old who had been found guilty of drunkenness offences on three occasions and for whom it was important to remain part of a friendship group of young men living on a housing estate where drinking was an important part of social life.

Mrs Cuxsom, aged 35, whose husband was the licensee of a public house in which it was necessary for her to work as a barmaid, had recently been ill with pancreatitis caused by her heavy drinking.

Mr Newsom, aged 30 years, an engineer officer in the merchant navy, had twice been refused permission to join his ship because of his drunkenness. He really enoyed a drink, and though he was worried about his future seemed unable to set reasonable limits to the amount he drank on any one occasion.

Mr Jopp, a 28 year old brewery worker, who had ready access to alcohol throughout his working day, had been demoted from his job as foreman because he was frequently so inebriated that he was unable to continue working. His wife was considering leaving him because of his drunken behaviour and because of the financial difficulties resulting from his demotion.

Miss Templeman, a 24 year old nurse, had recently had a car accident when driving whilst intoxicated and on one or two occasions had been unable to go to work because of alcohol induced gastritis. She was afraid her job might soon be in jeopardy if she did not reduce her drinking.

At an early stage in the life of the group the social worker designed a programme which enabled the conflict about saying 'no' to be explored, and then used techniques which enabled the clients to develop their capacity to be assertive. They simulated situations in which they were being pressed to take a drink, and through these learnt how to say 'no' without causing difficulty. Other aspects of the personal problems experienced by group members were easier to explore once they had some skill in handling the expectations others had that they would drink.

The range of social skills programmes that can be designed is limited only by the social worker's imagination and the resources on which he can call. Film, visiting speakers, pencil and paper exercises, dramatic reconstruction of incidents, and non-verbal exercises can all be used to good effect as long as the worker and group members are clear about the aims of the programme and consistently hold their goals at the centre of all their activities. Social skills groups can be fun, but the most careful preparation by the worker is necessary if the programmes are also to be effective.

Crisis intervention

The descriptions of problem solving and social skills training demonstrate that these methods require reflective thought on the part of the client and a capacity to commit himself to the planned, but relatively slow resolution of his difficulties. Some clients are in no state to engage in such a process with the worker at initial contact. The man who has killed a pedestrian whilst driving with more than the permitted level of alcohol in his blood stream, the women whose husband has left her, taking the children with him, because he can no longer tolerate her drunken behaviour and neglect of their home and children, or the person who has been made redundant following an interview with the company medical officer at which a diagnosis of alcoholism was made, may be in the state described by Rapoport (1965) as 'crisis' and unable to think or plan for himself. In Rapoport's definition a crisis is a temporary (no longer than six weeks), self-limiting state in which the individual's usual adaptive and problem solving abilities prove inadequate. It is an upset in the 'steady state' which the individual can maintain under normal circumstances through the purposeful use of his habitual problem-solving activities. Three inter-related factors produce crisis:

1. a threatening or hazardous event;
2. a symbolic link between this event and earlier experience

about which the individual still feels conflict or vulnerability; and
3. inability to respond with adequate coping mechanisms in the current situation.

The individual in crisis is incapacitated by anxiety and overwhelmed by helplessness; he is also likely to be in a state of cognitive confusion and in extreme cases demonstrates perceptual confusion. His behaviour is disorganised and often more concerned with the discharge of inner tension than with problem resolution (Rapoport 1970).

Clients in crisis are not always willing clients, and because of this and the seriousness of their situation they may have little hope of receiving help from the social worker. Those social work theorists and practitioners who have developed the crisis intervention approach to work, emphasise the importance in the first interview of focus, direction and engaging the client. The essence of crisis intervention is that it provides a rapid, helpful response to need and that the work will be completed through a small number (usually six or less) of contacts with the client. The worker will aim to correct the client's understanding of his situation, provide opportunity to verbalise feeling and discharge tension, so that a sense of autonomy can be regained, and make available whatever other resources are appropriate. The client will willingly engage in this work only when he is hopeful about the outcome. Consequently it is important for the worker to develop strategies designed to directly influence the level of hope and confidence in the client. Four such strategies are used by practitioners working with this method:

1. using the authority that stems from having specific knowledge and experience relevant to the crisis to offer useful information and direct appropriate advice;
2. relating positively and directly to the client, so that he knows his feelings are accepted, and then offering specific help to produce real (if slight) improvement in the situation;
3. showing confidence in the effectiveness of this approach to the problem; and
4. demonstrating commitment to helping the client and to working *with* him rather than *for* him.

It seems clear that this approach is consistent with what has been identified as important about working with clients who have alcohol problems. Crisis theory does not assume the client in crisis is sick, but rather that his normal coping capacities have temporarily failed under stress and that with help he will not only recover his old capacities but develop new ones. The crisis for all its pain and felt danger is perceived as a time when the client can, with support, maximise his potential for change and be responsive to the influence of others.

The worker using this method will be careful not to place too great responsibility for action on the client too soon, but will nevertheless invite his active involvement from the very beginning of contact. The directness of the worker's behaviour and the evidence of his commitment to helping will increase the client's sense of worth and encourage his interest in being involved in the resolution of his crisis. Initial contact with Mr Phillotson illustrates the use of crisis theory.

> Mr Phillotson, a batchelor aged 28 years, was admitted to hospital in emergency after taking an overdose. The social worker saw him a few hours later. He was tearful and hopeless about his future. Two weeks earlier he had been sacked from his job as a professional golfer because the quality of his performance had deteriorated as a result of his persistent excessive drinking. He had left the area because of his shame about this, and not daring to return to his family, had moved to a flat the rent of which he could not afford. The previous day he had been charged with shoplifting and was due to appear in court for an offence for which he knew he was guilty. The social worker did not minimise the seriousness of his situation but advised him to accept the offer made by the consultant to remain in hospital for another day. Mr Phillotson was anxious to make contact with his mother, but he was also afraid she would want nothing more to do with him. She had already been made angry by his excessive drinking and he thought the court appearance would cause his rejection. The worker quickly became aware that Mr Phillotson had a poor opinion of himself and she thought his anxiety about what would happen in court was out of proportion with the pettiness of what seemed to be a first offence. She concluded that a direct focus on this area would help Mr Phillotson to regain a more balanced perspective and so, with his agreement, took action to see he would be properly represented in court and made arrangements for the solicitor to see him in hospital the next morning. The social

> worker also made sure Mr Phillotson would have sufficient money to maintain himself during the first couple of weeks following discharge from hospital. Once he had met with the solicitor, Mr Phillotson began to be able to talk with the social worker about the extent to which his drinking was out of control and to think realistically about his immediate future.

In this case the social worker was moving towards the goals Rapoport (1970) suggests are achievable through the use of this method, that is: the relief of symptoms; restoration of the individual's optimal level of functioning; understanding the precipitating events; and identification of the remedial measures the individual can take. Rapoport suggests that it is sometimes also possible to help the client to recognise the origin of his current stresses in past experience and to assist him to initiate new ways of perceiving, thinking and feeling that allow him to begin developing new coping behaviours. In Mr Phillotson's case, movement towards these additional goals was possible.

The social worker visited Mr Phillotson the day after his discharge from hospital. At this, her third contact with him, he spoke of his lack of satisfaction with the sporting career he had pursued to please his parents and began to consider that his conflicts in this area had contributed to what he now saw as escape into drunkenness. At this stage Mr Phillotson and the social worker together established the short-term goals of finding temporary work, remaining abstinent for a month and making contact with his parents, and a longer term commitment to explore his situation and to identify ways by which he might increase his satisfaction and confidence in himself. This interview marked the end of the crisis intervention and movement into a phase in which other social work methods were used.

Working with the client who continues drinking

With the exception of Mr Whittle the clients discussed in this Chapter have been willing to try to control their drinking early in their contact with the social worker and have demonstrated an ability to modify their drinking behaviour. Only when control or abstinence has been achieved can the important issues on which long-term sobriety rests be dealt with. But some clients do not quickly control their drinking. Like Mr Whittle they repeatedly relapse into 'bingeing' or perhaps do not manage even intermittent sobriety.

In these circumstances it is important the social worker retains contact with the client without colluding with his uncontrolled behaviour and without reinforcing any sense of guilt or shame. Such clients can be very irritating. They arrive at the agency drunk and offensive; they may threaten violence; they fail to keep appointments; they telephone when the worker is engaged with other clients. Repeated behaviour of this sort makes colleagues, clerical staff and receptionists angry and upset, and produces negative feelings in the worker too. It is important to find practical ways of coping with the variety of situations that a drinking client precipitates which avoid rejection and hostility being directed at him and which maximise the possibility of changes in drinking behaviour being made.

If the client comes drunk to the agency it is probably advisable to postpone any attempt at serious discussion with him until the effects of intoxication have to some extent reduced. Some practitioners inform each client at initial contact that if he arrives at the agency drunk he will not be seen until he has sobered up. A private room in which a drunk client can wait is a useful agency resource, and a snack and a pot of tea are also helpful. Alternatively the client can be asked to take no further drink and to return at the end of the day or early next morning. Sometimes it may be appropriate to take the client to his home and to return there later to talk with him. The social worker should make clear to the client that it just is not possible for them to work on the issue with which he is concerned when he is drunk, but that he will help him to sober up so that discussion can take place later. This kind of exchange may have to be repeated several times before the client begins to establish sobriety. Archard (1979), in a study of homeless and habitual drunks, distinguishes the 'sober drunk' from the 'dry drunk'. ' "Dry drunks" are viewed as not having any conception of permanent sobriety' (p. 139) and are unable to make long-term plans. Archard argues that the 'dry drunk' is at an early phase in rehabilitation and that a sea change has to occur that moves the individual into being a 'sober drunk' who 'acquires a new personal psychology' and whose 'future orientation is directed at interests and activities lying beyond the skid-row world' (p. 139). Several shifts between uncontrolled drinking and being a 'dry drunk' may occur before the person is able to become a 'sober drunk' who can satisfactorily reintegrate into society.

The ability of the worker to continue to provide encouragement and support and to demonstrate patience and concern about repeated failure to maintain sobriety are crucial, and it may be useful for the client to link up with AA who can provide additional support. The client who continues uncontrolled drinking is unlikely to be able to learn to drink moderately and it will be helpful if the social worker is consistent in giving direct advice about achieving and maintaining abstinence. The worker should be most careful to avoid being drawn into a situation in which he colludes with such a client taking a drink. He should not, for example, join the client in the pub or permit him to drink from a bottle brought into the agency. It is essential to give the client every opportunity to take responsibility for his behaviour. 'Alcoholism is a game and a person can choose not to play' (Steiner 1971, p. 82), although of course, he may need a lot of help before he is able to hold to that choice.

Sometimes the client who continues drinking will refuse to see the worker or to accept referral to any other agency, but if that client continues to have contact with family or close friends there may still be a possibility of giving indirect help. The evidence seems to be that if the close family or people with whom the client lives are well informed about the effects of alcohol and understand the physical and emotional discomfort of the client, their approach to him will be positive and concerned; and that approach increases the likelihood of his coming to see the advantages of changing his drinking behaviour and modifying his lifestyle.

6 The Client's Family and Social Network

What use has patience,
Won with such difficulty?
Forced out in such a sigh?
from *Song of Patience* by Edwin Muir

The client's relationships with his nuclear and extended family, his neighbours, his friends and workmates, are all affected by a decision to change drinking behaviour (e.g. Mr Coney, p. 62), and without support within these relationships it is likely that sobriety will be abandoned, or that it will be maintained in the face of increasing stress and dissatisfaction. Mr Melbury provides an alarming example of the latter situation.

Mr Melbury, aged 55, was convinced by the evidence presented to him of his serious alcohol dependence. He made a decision to become abstinent and accepted admission to an ATU. He was active in in-patient group therapy and following discharge, six weeks later, joined an out-patient group, which he regularly attended for several months. He returned to his job as a foreman in an engineering works. He lived with his wife. His only child, a daughter, was married and lived a few miles distant, with her husband and two children.

Mr Melbury remained abstinent in the face of what he felt to be the derision of the people with whom he worked. His wife had an active social life and saw no reason either to include her husband in it or to make changes which would enable her to spend more time with him. She refused to see the social worker because, she said, 'I have no problems and my husband's problems are his own affair'. Mr Melbury was fond of his grandchildren, but anxious not to intrude on their family life, so visited them less often than he would have liked. He was more isolated and lonely than when he was drinking and saw no way of improving his situation. He refused to involve his daughter in any discussion because he thought it wrong to 'worry her'. He seemed to think his circumstances were a punishment for what he felt to be his years of neglect of his family. After remaining abstinent for nearly a year Mr Melbury committed suicide.

The involvement in the process of change of the significant people in the client's network is as important for clients who have alcohol problems as it is to other clients referred to practitioners in area teams, probation departments, hospitals and residential care.

The family

The spouse of the identified client

Until recently the great majority of clients referred because of alcohol problems were men; consequently the literature about spouses is almost exclusively about wives.

Twenty years ago the wives of people with alcohol problems were commonly described as 'driving their husbands to drink'; it was argued that psychopathology in the wife pre-dated the husband's alcohol problems (Whalen 1953; Lewis 1954). However, experience made it apparent that identifiable pathology in the wife was not invariably present before the emergence of the alcohol problems. A view suggesting that the behaviour demonstrated by wives (and other members of the family) could be explained in terms of their attempts to adjust to the difficulties imposed by living with someone whose drinking is out of control was promulgated (Lemert 1960; James and Goldman 1971).

Orford (1975) has pointed out that both these explanations of the interactions within marriages where one partner has an alcohol problem are over-simplications. He suggests that the interactions can be explained by the same concepts used to understand the marriages of other types of client who are under stress, and argues that it may be unhelpful to give emphasis to what is distinct about marriages where alcohol is a problem and more useful to concentrate on what is similar about all marriages in difficulty. The tendency to see alcohol problems as requiring specialist help may have resulted in the failure of practitioners to perceive the relevance of new, generally applicable methods of intervention. This seems to have been the reason for the slowness in recognising the potential of conjoint work and family therapy for helping families with alcohol related problems (Steinglass 1976: Janzen 1978).

The most useful framework for understanding a wife's behaviour and attitude in the face of her husband's alcohol problems would seem to be that of a complex system of interacting elements. The wife brings to the marriage her own expectations, conflicts and capacities, which interact with those of her partner and are affected by her experience of marriage and family relationships and of other activities in which she engages.

Although the available literature is largely concerned with wives, this interactionist approach is likely to be just as relevant to consideration of husbands whose wives have alcohol problems. It can also be concluded that husbands are as liable as wives to develop attitudes and behaviour which either make a change in the spouses' drinking difficult to achieve or fail to provide enough sources of satisfaction to make marriage enjoyable in abstinence. An understanding that this is the case and a willingness to make changes are crucial if the marriage is to continue and the partner is to achieve and maintain control of alcohol use. It is equally important for spouses to recognise that in taking responsibility for their own behaviour within the marital relationship they are not taking all the responsibility for causing their partners' alcohol problems. Exploration of the dynamics of interaction will enable the spouse to assess his commitment to his marriage and, if a decision is made to remain married, the spouse will be committed to act to modify his approach to the excessive drinking and to his relationship with his partner, and to assist the partner's attempts to change his drinking behaviour. Orford's data suggest that where the wife is critical of excessive drinking and asserts her views, but also demonstrates care and concern towards her husband, the alcohol dependent husband is more likely to achieve and maintain sobriety (Orford 1978). It seems that the spouse who is still positively engaged in the marriage is particularly helpful to the partner with an alcohol problem.

There are, however, some spouses who are thoroughly negative about their marriage and continue to be so although the partner has stopped drinking; the alcohol problems seem to be incidental to a basically unsatisfactory relationship. In these circumstances it may be appropriate for the marriage to end and for the social worker to support the client and his spouse through the ending process.

When assessing the situation it may be useful for the social worker to think about specific dimensions of marriage which seem to influence commitment to its satisfactory continuance. Levinger (1965) has proposed three dimensions.

1. *Attraction within marriage* This includes the respect and esteem of the spouse for his partner, sexual enjoyment within marriage, the extent to which their social lifestyle and economic circumstances are comfortable and attractive.
2. *Sources of barrier strength* These are the issues that force people to remain together although the relationship is a source

of frustration and unhappiness. They include feelings of obligation to the partner, the presence of dependent children, economic difficulties which would arise if the marriage ended, the attitudes of extended family and a moral and religious commitment to marriage.

3. *Sources of alternative satisfaction* Examples of these include a career that can be pursued independently, and the availability of a sexual partner who is preferred to the spouse.

These dimensions are common to all marriages: in marriages where one or both partners has an alcohol problem it may also be important to bear in mind that whilst excessive drinking is frequently described, especially by wives, as a source of unhappiness in marriage, sobriety is not usually perceived as a source of happiness. The fact of a partner's ability to maintain control of his drinking is not, therefore, certain to improve satisfaction within marriage although it will reduce dissatisfaction. It will certainly not be enough to rescue a marriage which has few attractions within it, where barriers to ending it are few and alternative sources of satisfaction available.

Children

Chapter 2 indicated that the children of a family where a parent has an alcohol problem are likely to experience stress and confusion. Teenagers may feel a great responsibility for keeping the family functioning and may have no legitimate outlet for their distress and resentment about their situation. The children of parents with severe alcohol problems may also become particularly confused, as our society is one in which attitudes to drinking and drunkenness are ambivalent and heavy drinking is a regular feature of life for many young adults. The teenager who has experience of the problems caused by alcohol abuse may have difficulty in developing a balanced perspective on alcohol use and in handling relationships with peers amongst whom regular drinking is common.

Any child growing up in a family where a parent is misusing alcohol will have experience of some of the problems which result and will have adapted to them. This adaptation may itself be a cause of discomfort if the parent gains control of his drinking and becomes active within the family.

> Dr Fitzpiers, a community physician, had two children, aged 9 and 11 years. They had learnt not to involve him in their activities and they avoided his company because of his unpredic-

> table drunken behaviour. Once his abstinence was established Dr Fitzpiers was eager to develop his relationship with his children and was hurt by their persistent resistance to his interest in them. Two interviews with the whole family enabled exploration of some of the difficulties and over the following months the relationship between the children and their father became more positive and active.

Quite small children have some awareness of the fact that drinking is the cause of peculiar behaviour in a parent, of family rows and of poverty, and they will usually be helped by the opportunity to join in some discussion and to develop their understanding.

> Mr and Mrs Durbeyfield were very unsure whether they should accept the social worker's advice to discuss Mr Durbeyfield's alcohol problem with their seven year old son. Mr Durbeyfield was admitted to hospital with hepatitis and suffered severe withdrawal symptoms for several days. Mrs Durbeyfield told George that 'Daddy is ill'. When George visited his father once the withdrawal symptoms had subsided he asked 'Don't you think you've been drinking too much? I think it is the drink that has made you ill'. George seemed untouched by the stigma associated with alcohol dependence; he was very matter-of-fact about the situation and quite able to cope with a conversation about it.

Denial and an attempt to cover up the facts would have confused George and suggested that alcohol dependence is shameful. It is important to recognise that children in families where a parent is abusing alcohol require special attention if they are to cope constructively (Cork 1969) and that the personal needs of the children are easily overlooked (Wilson and Orford 1978). When the support and advice of the social worker are available to them, parents will often provide all the help that is needed. However, the social worker should keep in mind the possibility that direct work with individual children or seeing the nuclear family as a group will be appropriate. A groupwork setting will be required by those teenagers who find the intensity of a person-to-person relationship with a social worker too difficult at a time when ambivalence about their parents has been exacerbated by alcohol problems and feelings of anger about adult authority are at their peak.

The child whose mother has an alcohol problem may be in particular need of help; it seems that fathers are not as well placed to protect a child from the serious consequences of alcohol abuse in the mother as mothers are to provide protection when father has an alcohol problem.

The extended family

There will be some clients for whom members of the extended family will be as important to their future adjustment as are the nuclear family. Mr Coney (Chapter 5) provides an example.

> Mr Coney's sons-in-law were important agents supporting his decision to remain abstinent. One of them was a docker and although he was not part of the same small work group as Mr Coney, he was a regular visitor to the Club, and knew Mr Coney's workmates. Both sons-in-law lived close by and formed part of the wider social network amongst whom Mr Coney had an established position. Once the two younger men understood the reasons for Mr Coney's behaviour they were ready to provide some protection and support, arranging to keep him company on some evenings and helping to reduce the pressure placed upon him to take a drink.

A number of clients do not live within a nuclear family structure and the social worker will have to consider the extent to which the involvement of other relatives is necessary. In some circumstances it may be important for the client that the social worker does not become active in work with his family.

> Mr Farfrae was a batchelor of 31 years. His parents, his older sister and her husband and his younger brothers had been constantly critical of him throughout the previous 15 years. His approach to life and his personal ambitions were very different from theirs. As a young man he had tried to justify his agnosticism and his lifestyle, but although he lived with his family most of that time he never felt accepted. In his late 20s he began to drink heavily, an activity that was particularly unacceptable to his abstinent Protestant family. A year before his referral to a hostel he had moved 150 miles from his family. As soon as he informed his family he was living in a hostel for people with alcohol problems the social worker received several telephone calls from family members offering to give background information and saying that he should return to his parents' home as soon as he left the hostel. Discussion with Mr Farfrae made it clear he needed to separate from his family. The social

worker and Mr Farfrae agreed she would reassure family members that he would be staying at the hostel for some weeks, but decline the offers to meet with her, and that Mr Farfrae would keep in touch with his parents by letter. It seemed more important for Mr Farfrae to demonstrate his independence as an adult than for the worker to have additional background information, and necessary for Mr Farfrae to develop greater self-esteem before trying to establish a closer relationship with members of his family.

In other situations the involvement of the social worker with the extended family may be crucial.

Mr Cawtree was the tenant of a small hill farm. He was a bachelor, and since his parents' deaths had shared his house with his two unmarried sisters who were a little older than he. Mr Cawtree had been a frail child and his sisters had grown up expecting him to need looking after. At 35 he was a heavily built, healthy man, running his own business, but was cosseted by his sisters. At the same time they expected him to escort them to social functions in the neighbourhood and to drink sociably. They were angry that his drinking was solitary and out of control, but did not find his suggestion that he become abstinent acceptable either. Nor did they find it easy to appreciate that Mr Cawtree might wish to have a social life somewhat separate from theirs. It seemed plain that Mr Cawtree could not achieve a satisfactory lifestyle for himself without some modification in his relationship with his sisters. Equally, it was clear he would continue to share his house with them. The social worker saw the sisters together twice. She gave them information about alcohol use as well as providing an opportunity for them to explore their discomfort and dissatisfaction with the current situation. Towards the end of the second interview it was possible to identify some concerns that they would like to explore in family interviews in which the worker met with them and Mr Cawtree together. During the course of several interviews it became possible for the three of them to negotiate changes in their approach to and expectations of each other, to implement these and to begin to express their feelings more directly.

Methods of work

A variety of approaches is available to the social work practitioner choosing to work with family members because they need help in their own right and/or because they play a key role in the identified client's plans for change. Detailed individual work with the client's spouse, drawing on the problem-solving method described in Chapter 5, may be appropriate, as may a similar approach with the teenage children of the client. Family therapy is sometimes advocated, and so is conjoint work with the client and his spouse. Some practitioners work with groups of spouses and it has been suggested that couples' groups (i.e. groups composed of perhaps five identified clients and their spouses) may provide effective help. It is clearly important to try to identify criteria which help to simplify the choice of method of intervention. Three types of situation are likely to be most appropriately approached on a person-to-person basis, at least in the first instance.

1. The spouse of the identified client is sometimes so demoralised and undermined by the chaos of the situation caused by the client's excessive drinking that it is necessary for the social worker to provide an individual supportive relationship within which he can re-establish a positive sense of identity and competence.

> Mr Fawley had returned home every night for more than two years in a grossly intoxicated state. He lived a life increasingly separate from his wife and their five young children. He stayed in bed until mid-day, and began drinking as soon as he rose. He went to his newspaper sub-editor's job in mid-afternoon, returning home again in the early hours of the morning. He seldom seemed to eat and was becoming increasingly careless of his appearance. He was often physically sick when he returned home and Mrs Fawley had moved from the marital bed because he had become incontinent. Mr Fawley was irritable and tremulous if his alcohol supply was reduced. A normally extrovert and amusing man who encouraged and supported his shy, diffident wife, he had become physically repulsive, querulous and prone to unprovoked outbursts of rage. His drinking caused considerable financial hardship and there was anxiety about his capacity to continue to hold down his job. Mrs Fawley felt alone and unsupported in circumstancs that overwhelmed her. She thought she might be in some way to blame for the situation and felt guilty about the resentment and revulsion with which she sometimes regarded her husband. The social worker met with Mrs Fawley each week and within a supportive relationship enabled her to identify how *she* might improve the family's

situation and to develop confidence in her own abilities to take practical and effective action.

Sometimes the teenage children of a client may need similar individual help.

For example, 15 year old John had grown up expecting fierce arguments between his parents on Friday and Saturday nights when his father returned home drunk. Sometimes there had been fights in which he had to intervene to protect his mother from his father's attacks. He knew the family were in financial difficulties because of his father's drinking, and although he had wanted to stay on at school, he began to feel he would have to leave and get a job as soon as possible. John became miserable and withdrawn; he had few friends and had started to truant. He resented the position in which he felt his parents placed him, yet was fond of them both and wanted to be helpful. At the point when his father accepted help from the local council on alcoholism it was clear that John needed access to someone outside the family with whom he could explore his feelings about his parents and learn to adjust to the differences his father's sobriety made to family life. The social worker was particularly important in helping John to accept that his crucial role as mediator between his parents had become unnecessary and that he was no longer his mother's closest confidant.

2. A spouse may sometimes have a long-lasting personal problem which exists independently of the client's alcohol problem, but which may create additional stress for a client struggling to remain sober.

Mrs Dollery was a tense, demanding woman constantly prone to interpret trivial incidents as in some way sinister. Mr Dollery had coped with the difficulties this caused by being extremely protective of his wife and readily responding to her demands. He had been a heavy drinker all his adult life and heavy, regular drinking had eventually escalated into severe alcohol dependence and cirrhosis of the liver. He accepted the need to maintain abstinence but found his wife's behaviour difficult to cope with. The social worker offered regular contact with Mrs Dollery on a long-term basis with the aim not only of relieving the strain on Mr Dollery in the early months of abstinence and providing a supportive relationship for Mrs Dollery, but also of providing Mrs Dollery with an alternative model for interpreting and dealing with the mundane incidents which caused her such distress.

3. Where the client's spouse and/or children are negative and unco-operative careful individual work may be necessary if family members are to work through their anger and develop positive relationships.

> Mr Creedle was angry with his wife for what he described as causing him 'needless trouble'. He could see no reason why she should drink to excess and rejected her explanation that she was lonely and oppressed by the repeated moves made necessary because of his frequent postings as a regular soldier. Mr Creedle scarcely accepted his wife's need of social work help, and saw no reason at all why he should be bothered by requests from the worker to come to see him. He regarded Mrs Creedle's inability to drink 'sensibly' as an indicator of personal weakness and gave the impression of being undermined by his inability to control her. Only after several months of careful individual work, during which his wife became increasingly well-established in sobriety, and regained some of her competence and liveliness, was Mr Creedle willing to meet with the social worker, Mrs Creedle and her counsellor to consider how each partner's sense of satisfaction with the marriage relationship might be increased.

Individual work with the spouse of the identified client may be a preliminary to seeing the marriage partners together. Conjoint interviews in which the married partners come together with one or two workers have been a feature of the Institute of Marital Studies approach since the 1960s (Family Discussion Bureau 1962; Mattinson and Sinclair 1980), and have been found to be a useful method of working with marriage partners when one of them has an alcohol problem. The method is often used in conjunction with individual interviews with the partners, with conjoint interviews planned at intervals during the process of change and adjustment, and providing the means by which the differing perspectives of the marriage partners can be brought together. A separate worker may be allocated to each of the two partners and in individual interviews problems and expectations are explored. The two workers keep in close touch about the directions their interviews are taking and, in conjunction with the marriage partners, plan occasions when the four of them meet. In these meetings progress can be assessed, differences explored, goals established and the means of achieving them agreed. Intermittent, regular meetings of the four people involved are particularly useful for:

1. providing the practitioners with direct experience of the interaction between partners;
2. providing a structure within which the couple can safely explore issues that normally feel too dangerous or upsetting to raise. In the conjoint interview the presence of the worker who has a special understanding of each partner ensures that neither partner will feel too exposed to attack nor too susceptible to isolation and misunderstanding;
3. increasing the partners' awareness and understanding of each other through making appropriate connections between feelings, attitudes and behaviours; and
4. enabling the workers to demonstrate effective ways of raising and resolving difficulties, showing concern and so on, and thus providing an alternative model for the couple.

Mr and Mrs Fawley (see p. 89) provide an example of the use of conjoint work.

> Mr Fawley eventually accepted referral to a psychiatrist. He reluctantly accepted the need to become abstinent and in weekly interviews with the psychiatrist began tentatively to explore some of his difficulties. Mrs Fawley continued to see the social worker and supported her husband in his attempt to maintain abstinence in spite of his urge to drink. She moved back to the marital bed in spite of her anxiety about a further pregnancy (the couple were Roman Catholic) as the incontinence ceased and she felt it important to demonstrate her wish to show care and concern. Mr Fawley remained withdrawn, offering very little relationship with the children and apparently not noticing the severe financial difficulties of the family. After six weeks' abstinence a conjoint interview took place in which it was possible for the marriage partners to share some of their hopes and expectations of their relationship and to express concern and understanding to each other. A further meeting, four weeks later, took place at a point when both Mr and Mrs Fawley were a little more secure and confident about themselves as individuals, and focused more directly upon some of their frustrations and difficulties within their relationship, as well as on the practical and urgent matters arising from their financial problems. A third conjoint interview four weeks later enabled the couple to discuss a one-day drinking spree of Mr Fawley's, and then to offer help to each other with some of their specific personal and

> practical difficulties. In two further conjoint sessions Mr and Mrs Fawley began to express some pleasure to each other about the developments within their relationship and to seriously discuss their 11 year old son's difficulties at school. Weekly individual contact continued between the conjoint interviews, so that specific personal issues could be addressed. Mr Fawley needed particular help in maintaining abstinence at times of stress and frustration and in adjusting his hopes and expectations for himself; Mrs Fawley discussed the possibility of seeking contraceptive advice, and explored her ambivalence about the Church and her difficulties in coping with authority and dependence.

In this example the social worker worked in collaboration with a psychiatrist, but in other instances the co-workers might both be social workers. What is crucial is not the discipline from which the workers come, but their ability to work closely together in a situation where they share responsibility. This sharing will only be possible if they are able freely to discuss their individual work with the respective partners, and to examine together their identification with the marriage partner with whom they work and the extent to which the partners' relationship is reflected in their own interactions.

The reasons presented to support the view that a groupwork setting is often the most likely to help the spouses of identified clients are similar to those (outlined in Chapter 5) used in respect of the problem drinkers. The support (and challenge) of other people in similar positions seem especially important. A spouse quite often believes that no one else understands or is experiencing chaos, unhappiness or fear similar to his own and feels a sense of relief when he meets other people coping with similar situations. The intimacy and camaraderie that group membership offers can reduce feelings of isolation and provide security within which to explore how to take action to improve the situation. Within a group of spouses members will also be quick to appreciate the difficulties of coping with a marriage partner who is drinking excessively and to identify the secondary gains that continued uncontrolled drinking provides. Spouses, like problem drinkers, experience the stigma attached to uncontrolled drinking and its consequences. Mrs Edlin, describing her situation in retrospect, said 'I was not the estimable, valued person I had worked so hard to appear. I was unacceptable; I was nothing in the eyes of our society'. Sensitivity to the potential criticism and rejection of friends and neighbours often prompts a spouse to try to keep secret what is happening, so membership of a group may be particularly helpful in providing an accepting and supportive environment in which anxiety and distress about what is happening can be expressed.

A range of methods of groupwork may be employed by the social worker. The aim should be to match the method with the goals for the group. For some groups the primary goal may be to reduce the sense of isolation of spouses. The group may then centre around some social activity and always be open for new members to join. Other groups will aim to focus directly on personal problems and may be closed (i.e. have constant membership throughout the life of the group). The available literature on social groupwork can be used to help with the matching of goals, structure, methods and techniques (e.g. Lowry 1970; Hartford 1972; Roberts and Northen 1976; Brown 1979).

It cannot be assumed that all spouses whose marriage partner is abusing alcohol and who would be helped through membership of a group can be brought together in the same group, and it will be necessary to give careful consideration to the selection of members. The worker should also consider whether it is helpful for a group of wives to work together and whether a male or female social worker is the more appropriate leader. If the group is to be composed of both husbands and wives, it will be important to pay attention to the balance between sexes and to the potential for pairing that such a group offers.

The following account of membership of a group for the wives of men admitted to an ATU gives an indication of what it might be possible to achieve through groupwork, as well as demonstrating some of the difficulties in successfully leading a group. The group member who provided this account had several months of regular individual contact with a social worker before joining the group.

> 'You can say anything you like' was the main introduction to the group, and our leader, while talking so that we got to know him and to feel support, said little, answered few questions, interpreted some of what we said and summed up at the end of the meeting the directions the talk had taken. 'The wives of the men we see have been found to be generally very competent people.' This was one of the few leads we were given, and most wives found it all just as perplexing as I did. Tell us, put us in the picture, advise us, . . . surely you are not asking us to consider

ourselves? I could help here, knowing some of the complexities of interaction between husbands and wives by this time; but what I said was threatening, and I found myself very anxious when I saw hostility aroused. I began to understand my limitations and ambivalence. Personal foibles were common to us all and revealing them was part of the purpose of the group.

There was a large turnover of wives. A minority stayed the course. Continuing with membership seemed to depend upon whether one could bear to turn the light upon oneself. Some came only at times of great crisis. Some came, but even over many sessions were doubtful if it 'did any good'. Some were ready to be analytical, could abstract and could understand something of the interaction occurring. Some learnt just enough to move away from thinking of alcohol abuse as a moral problem. One or two of us actually loosed off some very angry feelings and felt the better for it. I think the group situation is good because people can be doing and seeing on all sorts of different levels at the same time: the same subject reached different ears with different sounds.

Sometimes we were trivial and engaged in tea-party talk, although we found it unsatisfying. One member used subtly to divert onto another subject whenever we appeared to be going below the surface. At other times we were drawn, without self-consciousness, into support and intense feelings for one person's particular crisis. We could never underestimate the seriousness of alcohol abuse nor the likelihood of 'slips' – broken lives lay all around us. But steadiness and stability increased as time passed. New wives could see a core of 'older wives' happy, making plans, talking about persons and not bottles, leading ordinary, even respected, lives.

At times the eternal coming and going of members was frustrating, however, as new members often took us back to old issues. New wives seemed to want to tell their story and voice resentments, deeply bottled up feelings. It was difficult to appreciate that we were describing our feelings, not simply our husbands' actions: the feelings resided in us and their nature said something about us. We seemed both to feel something and deny the feeling, to feel ill-done by and to need to feel ill-done by. We were encouraged to express our feelings, slowly and tentatively, and this led the way out of the impasse.

> I left the group about a year after joining it – it seemed time. I announced one week that I was leaving after the following week's meeting and was surprised to find that the leader was proposing to divide the group into older and more recent members. Was this an invitation to stay? Nevertheless, 'I really think I must go'. Later, I talked about it to a friend who had been a group member. She said that they hadn't seemed able to say they wanted me to stay, and had felt very empty for some time. That prompted further whirring of the kaleidoscope: the work does not end with the end of the group. However, I felt no need to join another group.

The teenage children of the identified client may be more effectively helped through membership of a group than through individual contact with the social worker as they are at an age when peer group relationships and influence are particularly important, and yet may have an acute sense of isolation. The opportunity to meet with a group of others may not only be reassuring and supportive to the young person because it reveals the similarity between his situation and that of others, it also fosters his ability to develop relationships with people of his own age and provides a basis from which he can develop his own social network. A group for the teenage children of identified clients is likely to be most effective when it meets frequently over a comparatively short period of time (i.e. two to three months). It is probably not helpful to young people if their activities and thinking become too closely identified with alcohol abuse.

The interaction between alcohol abuse and family members has two aspects. On the one hand, the excessive use of alcohol by one family member will create financial, social and emotional problems for other members of the family. On the other hand, as time passes alcohol abuse becomes a factor built into the functioning of the family, so that although a change in drinking behaviour is desirable it is also threatening to the equilibrium of the family which has developed a pattern of interaction that is in some ways dependent on the continuance of alcohol abuse.

> Members of Mrs Stannidge's family had taken over aspects of her role whilst she remained incompetent and incoherent. Like a small child, she was protected and cared for by her husband and older daughter; her younger daughter and son shared the cooking and household chores, and Mr Stannidge managed the family budget. The family seemed to have functioned very

> comfortably in this way, and family members were quite negative about the changes Mrs Stannidge initiated when she became abstinent.

Since alcohol problems are so clearly family problems, it seems logical to consider that where the identified client's family is intact, working with the family as a group may be the most effective method of social work intervention. In recent years it has become clearer that family therapy is an approach that can be particularly effective in enabling change and providing individual family members with the scope for growth that they need. A number of highly skilled and original workers have developed a variety of methods of family therapy. British psychiatrists and social workers have been amongst the methodological innovators (Walrond-Skinner 1976; Skynner 1976) and specialists in the field of alcohol studies (Steinglass 1976) have begun to advocate these methods of intervention in families where alcohol abuse is a problem. The planned use of family therapy may include work with individuals and with sub-groups as well as with the family as a whole. A range of techniques may be called upon, such as sculpting, role-play and role reversal and the assignment of tasks to be carried out between meetings. The focus in all the methods within this approach is on current relationship, interaction and structure; historical material may be introduced by family members, but is used to clarify current concerns.

Family groupwork may be of real value where the member abusing alcohol is a son or daughter, as well as where it is one of the marriage partners.

> Billy, aged 17 years, was placed on probation after being found guilty of taking and driving a car whilst disqualified and when his blood alcohol level was above the legal limit. During preparation of the Social Inquiry Report the probation officer became aware of the seriousness of Billy's drinking problem and of the hostility of family members to what was described by them as irresponsible and disgusting behaviour. Once he was placed on probation it emerged that Billy felt himself an outsider within his own family: he was always in the wrong. The family consisted of Billy's parents and his two sisters, aged 20 years and 15 years. The probation officer arranged to see them together in their home. It quickly emerged that Billy could indeed do nothing right: everyone's anger and irritation was lodged in him and he responded with delinquent or unacceptable behaviour

that reinforced the others' view of him. No-one noticed that he was miserable and ashamed of his unemployed status and his efforts to help with household chores were misunderstood by his mother. It was also noticeable that family members seldom listened to each other, and that 15 year old Sue seemed to be entirely ignored at times.

During the course of subsequent family interviews it began to be possible to identify some of the hopes and expectations of individual family members. The probation officer encouraged them to explore how they might go some way to meeting these for each other. He introduced role reversal as a means of helping them tune into each other's feelings and experience and encouraged them to experiment with new ways of relating to each other. Over a period of several months Billy reduced his use of alcohol and no longer came home drunk, abusive and physically sick. During the same period his father began to show more interest in him and to be less belligerent towards him. Sue still seemed tense and withdrawn but her older sister was beginning to draw her into family activities.

This example demonstrates that it is not necessary to have access to elaborate resources before undertaking family therapy. The probation officer was aware of the potential disadvantages of seeing the family at home – he would be a guest in their house, the television, if switched on, would be a distraction and the appearance of a neighbour might disrupt the interviews. However, he had concluded that family members were neither secure enough nor hopeful enough to make the effort to come to the probation department. He discussed the use of family interviews with them, and negotiated the time of visits and the presence of everyone. From the second interview the television was switched off as soon as the six of them were assembled.

It is increasingly common for social workers in a variety of agencies to make contact with clients abusing alcohol whilst their families are still intact and before severe dependence has been established. Clients are likelier to achieve control of their drinking if they have an intact family whose members are willing to actively engage with them in the process of solving their alcohol related problems, and the various forms of family therapy may be particularly effective methods of achieving family participation.

The wider social network

Employers and workmates

In a number of the examples already quoted the significance of the client's working situation has been apparent, either because behaviour there had been a cause of difficulty (e.g. Mrs Charmond in Chapter 3, Mr Clare in Chapter 5) or because of the pressure to drink within the work situation (e.g. Mr Coney, Mr South and other members of his social skills group). Often clients will take action to deal with these difficulties themselves. Sometimes the only help they need is an opportunity to discuss the difficulties and to rehearse how they will approach them. However, some clients are too insecure to present their own case to a manager or employer, especially if the employer's attitude suggests he is only willing to listen to a person in authority and with expertise. The worker should, therefore, be willing to make appropriate contacts with employers and managers, using the telephone and direct personal contact. It may be helpful to make use of printed information that provides a straightforward description of alcohol problems. The National Council on Alcoholism and health education groups publish attractive, easy to read pamphlets which are readily available and can be left for the employer to read at leisure, once the worker has pointed out the most relevant sections.

Clearly the social worker will have to be careful to clarify with the client what he is willing to have the worker share with his employer or manager and to ensure the employer accepts that any discussion is confidential. However, it may be helpful to the client for his employer to know that social work help will continue to be available.

There is still a poor level of understanding of alcohol problems in our society and although some large companies have begun to develop policies which ensure the appropriate handling of situations in which an employee's alcohol problems intrude into the social work situation, the majority have not. It may be that through a sensitive approach to the circumstances of a particular employee the social worker can demonstrate the usefulness of collaboration between employer and helping agencies, and the potential advantages of a general policy describing the way in which the company intends alcohol problems amongst its employees will be approached.

Occasionally the workmates or colleagues of identified clients are a crucial influence.

Mr Longways worked in a small iron foundry. He was part of a team of men who moulded, dressed and finished heavy iron work. The work was exhausting, hot and dirty and it was customary for the team to take a drink at the end of the day. Mr Longways had been subject to anger and criticism because of his excessive lunchtime drinking. He presented a danger to himself and others when drunkenness interfered with his competence: his rate of production was also reduced and other members of the team had to take some of his share of the work in order to ensure the team's wage level was maintained. When Mr Longways' general practitioner referred him to an ATU he was assessed as severely alcohol dependent and advised to remain abstinent. When he returned to his work team Mr Longways experienced as much hostility about his abstinence as there had previously been about his drunkenness and felt he could not go on coping with it. He accepted the social worker's offer to meet his shop steward to discuss the nature of alcohol dependence and ways in which Mr Longways' work situation might be made more comfortable.

Friends and neighbours

Currently social workers seldom plan direct work with the friends and neighbours of a client, although increasingly they understand the significance of the social network to a wide range of social problems referred to them. It does sometimes happen that when the worker visits a client at home a friend may also be present, and a few agencies encourage local residents to make use of agency facilities (e.g. for cooking or washing) on a regular daily basis. These circumstances may offer opportunities to increase friends' or neighbours' understanding and willingness to help the client, but these are serendipitous occurrences rather than elements of planned programmes of social work.

Two planned means of increasing the understanding of neighbours and friends and mobilising their help may be employed. The client who feels unsupported or excluded amongst his friends and neighbours as a result of his drinking problems may be invited to identify the people in his social network who are most important to him and, if he is unable to consider talking to them himself, the worker might arrange to visit at a time when he can meet the key people with the express aim of helping them to be better informed about alcohol problems, to understand better their friend's difficulty and to identify ways of helping him (Rueveni 1979).

The second means is less direct. The social worker can seek out key people within a neighbourhood (e.g. the minister, the local councillor) with the aim of demonstrating the importance of an informed approach to alcohol problems. Further, local groups and organisations can be visited and information given about the nature of alcohol problems and the ways in which people coping with them can be helped. This kind of activity is often not popular amongst social workers, perhaps because the effort required is considerable and the impact uncertain. However, it is suggested that more concerted activity in a neighbourhood, planned in collaboration with specialist alcohol agencies, such as local councils on alcoholism, with health educationists and professionals from other disciplines, such as general practitioners and guidance teachers, may be particularly useful in shifting opinion about alcohol abuse in general and about specific members of the local community in particular.

This kind of social work involvement within the local community should prompt practitioners to reflect upon attitudes to alcohol and alcohol problems amongst the general public and amongst those involved in the development of social and economic policy (Kendell 1979) and might serve to increase their interest in the means by which the development of alcohol problems might be prevented.

7 Developing Policy and Practice

> As we grow older
> The world becomes stranger, the pattern more complicated
> from *Four Quartets* by T. S. Eliot

Two factors given emphasis throughout this book are basic to the future development of policy and practice.

1. A range of varied services is needed to meet the varied requirements of clients. As the Royal College of Psychiatrists (1979) has pointed out, 'Causes of excessive drinking are always multiple and interactive and therefore any single factor model of causation is not only wrong in theory, but in practice will lead to inappropriate responses to the individual' (p. 22). Glaser *et al.* (1978) describe the situation as one requiring agencies to develop a polychromatic system of alternative forms of help, rather than a monochromatic system of similar programmes (p. 219).

2. It is neither appropriate nor necessary to wait until severe dependence has been reached before intervening to help arrest or resolve alcohol related problems. Indeed it is more logical to assume that the earlier the intervention is made the more likely is it that the problems can be resolved. A specialist treatment service which 'sits back and waits for the problem to present itself as "alcoholism" will only be able to make a tiny contribution to what is really needed' (Royal College 1979, p. 87).

The report of the Kessell Committee on *The Pattern and Range of Services for Problem Drinkers* (Advisory Committee on Alcoholism 1978) emphasises that it is necessary (1) to involve primary care agents, such as general practitioners and social workers, in the development of a comprehensive (polychromatic) system of care for clients with alcohol problems and (2) to find ways of structuring that system that encourage collaboration between all the primary care and specialist agents involved. The phrase 'system of care' has particular relevance since services have often developed haphazardly and tend to offer 'a cluttered, disjointed, overlapping unco-ordinated set of programs that are opportunistic and responsive primarily to an immediate crisis or to community tension' (Holder and Stratas 1972). This is likely to result in imbalance in the range of facilities offered, and insufficient flexibility to take account both of the changes that occur over time in the population in need of help, and of the implications of research evidence about what methods of intervention are most effective in enabling clients to resolve alcohol related problems.

Collaboration to provide a system of care

Collaboration is necessary at two levels:

1. at the level of policy and decision making about the allocation of agency resources; and
2. amongst practitioners in the statutory and voluntary agencies in health, education and social services who are providing direct service to clients.

Social workers are now familiar with the difficulties inherent in interdisciplinary and inter-agency collaboration. The dynamics of interaction that are a well recognised aspect of work with non-accidental injury to children (Hallett and Stevenson 1980) and of psychiatric hospital care (Hunt 1979) are also a feature of work with clients presenting alcohol problems (Cook 1975). The commitment and persistence of both senior managers and practitioners will be as necessary to effective collaboration in work with clients with alcohol problems as it is proving to be in other spheres.

It seems that the suggestion, made in the Kessel Committee Report, to extend the existing Joint Care Planning system may be the most appropriate means of ensuring the co-ordination of policy and planning in the development of services in England and Wales (in Scotland the parallel system of Joint Liaison is less well developed, but has the potential to become a means through which a rational system of policy and planning can emerge). The Kessel Report recommends that 'each Joint Care Team set up a specialist sub-group to review and make recommendations on services for problem drinkers' (para. 4.35) and goes on to emphasise the importance of extending membership of these specialist sub-groups to representatives of voluntary agencies as well as the usual representatives from the health and social service authorities. If a truly comprehensive system of complementary services is to develop it will also be essential to incorporate representatives from probation and after-care (in England and Wales) and education departments. A formal structure like Joint Care Planning, which can bring together key local planners and those who control the allocation of resources, may be the system most likely to facilitate the action necessary for the development of a comprehensive and rational set of facilities in a locality but little guidance is available on how to create and implement jointly formulated plans, and much rests on the skill and commitment of senior staff in all the agencies involved in a particular locality.

The importance of matching service to client need is discussed in Chapter 4 and has been reported in a number of studies (e.g. Chafetz and Keller 1974, Polich *et al.* 1980). Only through collaboration amongst practitioners in direct contact with clients will it be possible to ensure that each client reaches the services most likely to help him. Practitioners in the voluntary and statutory agencies of a locality will aid collaboration if they can come together as a resource group and agree what range of service they will provide. It will be important that practitioners keep in mind the notion that the provision of truly different regimes and the scrupulous matching of individuals to facilities is likely to improve the results of the service system as a whole. They need to be aware that the different facilities run by any one agency tend to become similar in approach and so provide fewer real alternative forms of care than can several different agencies. The dominance of one approach to helping tends to define the kinds of clients who are offered help within inappropriately narrow parameters. This difficulty was demonstrated in the too-narrow focus of ATUs in the late 1960s (see Chapter 1).

Emphasis on early intervention, and on the importance of a system of service designed to meet the needs of a particular locality, draws attention to the advantages which can accrue from close collaboration between specialist workers (such as those in ATUs) and the generalist primary care agents (such as local authority social workers and probation officers). The ability of the latter groups to identify alcohol over-use and to provide appropriate help for clients can be greatly enhanced when support and consultation are available from the specialists. Appreciation of this point has led to the suggestion that a Community Alcohol Team (CAT) could usefully be developed in each locality (Shaw *et al.* 1978). The team would be composed of a social worker, a psychiatrist, and perhaps individuals from other disciplines, such as nursing or clinical psychology. All the members of the CAT would have detailed knowledge and experience of clients with alcohol problems. Team members would make themselves available for consultation with social workers, general practitioners and so on, and thus enable the primary care agents to develop their capacity to provide help for clients with alcohol problems and ensure the ready availability of special medical or nursing care for those needing it. Clearly the development of this kind of inter-agency and interdisciplinary consultation is dependent on willing collaboration amongst practitioners and a joint commitment to extension and improvement of service for clients with alcohol problems. Although the Kessel Committee Report advocates the development of CATs along the lines suggested by Shaw and his colleagues, it does not address the difficult questions about which agency should take the initiative in establishing the team; nor those about its accountability and management. These questions will have to be satisfactorily resolved if the CAT is to emerge as a useful component in the system of care. It will not, in any case, be a practical possibility in all areas of the country. There are insufficient skilled specialists and they are unevenly distributed geographically, so it is not feasible to achieve this close working relationship everywhere. It will, therefore, be necessary for some social work agencies to look for alternative systems of support and consultation to counteract any lack of confidence and competence amongst practitioners.

Developing an appropriate continuum of care

As knowledge of what constitutes the most effective system of care is incomplete, it is important that those involved in developing a continuum of care keep in mind the need to adapt and change the available services as research and practice demonstrate methods of increasing effectiveness in the resolution of specific alcohol problems.

Flexibility is also necessary to take account of changes in the population of clients with alcohol problems. For example, during recent years the number of women with serious problems has increased (see Chapter 1) so that now more than a third of people seen at alcohol treatment clinics and local councils on alcoholism are women, yet hostel and half-way house facilities have not developed to take account of the increased need amongst women. Similarly, the number of young people who are misusing alcohol is increasing (Plant 1981), yet the educational and personal counselling available to them seldom seems to focus on alcohol use; there are few examples of provision like that in one part of Scotland where a psychologist offers a social skills programme to young people who have committed offences whilst under the influence of alcohol. Again, it seems that little attention has been given to services for elderly people who over-use alcohol, although the staffs of elderly persons' homes express concern about drinking by residents from time to time, and occasional papers appear (e.g. Merry 1980) indicating that the problem may be significant and that there may be a need for special provision.

As the system of care extends to take account of newly recognised needs, it will be important to keep the correct balance between services. For example, in recent years there has been growing awareness of the need for help of homeless and vagrant problem drinkers who are frequently, and inappropriately, sentenced to short terms of imprisonment. However, two factors have to be kept in mind whilst planning services for this group within a rational system of care. Firstly, some of the needs of habitual drunken offenders can best be met through the improvement of facilities for all homeless persons, and secondly, although homeless habitual drunken offenders constitute approximately 2 per cent of all those who have alcohol problems in Great Britain as a whole (Royal College 1979), they may form a disproportionately large number of the problem drinkers in specific districts of some towns.

During the process of developing a systematic approach to a continuum of care, other demographic factors should emerge as significant influences on the structure and setting of services offered and the client groups to be given priority in a particular locality. That the range and structure of service appropriate in a highly urbanised and densely populated area, such as Birmingham, needs to be radically different from that of a large, rural and sparsely populated area, such as the Highland Region of Scotland, may be obvious. But less obvious factors such as the pattern of public transport services and the nature of locally available employment may also be of importance.

Other differences associated with variations in cultural attitudes, expectations and behaviour will be relevant considerations. O'Connor's study (1978) of English, Irish and Anglo-Irish young people demonstrates one significant dimension of these differences. She shows that socio-cultural issues, such as the customs and patterns of drinking within an ethnic group, the social meaning and function of alcohol, the social rules of drinking and peer group support for heavy drinking, are significant influences on alcohol use amongst young people. O'Connor suggests that ethnic and cultural factors interact with other important variables, such as the young person's exposure to heavy drinking and the attitudes of his parents, to determine drinking behaviour. Any service established to encourage the wise use of alcohol or to enable those already misusing alcohol to modify their pattern of drinking seems likely to be effective only when its design takes full account of cultural factors.

The availability of national and local resources will constitute further and powerful influences on those planning services and may prompt opportunistic rather than systematic service development. For example, the availability of a pool of skilled specialist nurses at a local hospital, or the presence of a voluntary agency with the capacity and interest to develop residential services may be a significant influence. Similarly, the availability of central government funding will act to stimulate the development of special types of service. The fact that the funding that has been available for new hostel projects in England and Wales (DHSS Circular 21/73) ceased in 1980 is likely to encourage a reappraisal of the need for additional hostels. It may also prompt further consideration of the use of sheltered housing projects for which funding may be more readily available, and, if residential facilities become increasingly difficult to finance, practitioners and planners may wish to encourage the development of day care services.

Specialist and generalist agencies will require the ability to tolerate diversity and to think imaginatively if the most effective continuum of care for a particular locality is to be available. They will also require skill and determination in holding to a rationally thought out scheme for developing services.

The Kessel Committee emphasised the importance of social workers in voluntary agencies, probation departments and local authority departments, but it did not clarify what their contribution should be. Clarity is now needed and the ability of social work practitioners to articulate their views is crucial if effective social work services for clients with alcohol problems are to form part of a continuum of care. Only if practitioners convey to the managers and planners in their agencies detailed, accurate information and the conclusions they draw from it will it be possible to think through what contribution social work can make now and what initiatives agencies should be taking in the future. One social work agency has begun to articulate its policy in relation to people with alcohol problems and is examining the implications of that policy for training, practice and agency priorities (Strathclyde 1978) but further work is required by employing agencies, social work educators, and, most of all, by involved practitioners, if the capacity of social workers to help people with alcohol problems is to be fully developed.

References

Adelstein, A. and White, G. (1976), *Alcoholism and Mortality in Population Trends*, no. 6, London, HMSO

Advisory Committee on Alcoholism, (1977), *Report on Prevention*, London, DHSS and Welsh Office

Advisory Committee on Alcoholism Report, (1978), *The Pattern and Range of Services for Problem Drinkers*, London, DHSS and Welsh Office

Aitken, P. (1978), *Ten to 14 year olds and Alcohol*, Edinburgh, HMSO

Alibrandi, L. (1978), 'The Folk Psychotherapy of Alcoholics Anonymous' in Zimberg, S., Wallace, J. and Blume, S. (eds.), *Practical Approaches to Alcoholism Psychotherapy*, New York, Plenum Press

Archard, P. (1979), *Vagrancy, Alcoholism and Social Control*, London, Macmillan Press

Armor, D., Polich, J. and Stambul, H. (1978), *Alcoholism and Treatment*, Chichester, John Wiley & Sons

Birchmore, D. F. and Walderman, R. L. (1975), 'The woman alcoholic: a review', *The Ontario Psychologist*, vol. 7, no. 3

Bott, E. (1957), *Family and Social Network*, London, Tavistock Publications

Bromet, E. and Moos, R. (1979), 'Prognosis of alcoholic patients: comparisons of abstainers and moderate drinkers', *British Journal of Addictions*, vol. 74, no. 2, pp. 183–8

Brown, A. (1979), *Groupwork*, London, Heinemann Educational Books

Cartwright, A. K. J., Harwin, J., Shaw, S. and Spratley, T. (1977), *Implementing a Community Response to Problems of Alcohol Abuse*, London, Maudsley Alcohol Pilot Project

Cartwright, A. K. J., Shaw, S. and Spratley, T. (1975), *Designing a Comprehensive Community Reponse to Problems of Alcohol Abuse*, London, Maudsley Alcohol Pilot Project

Chafetz, M. and Keller, M. (eds.), (1974), *Alcohol and Health, New Knowledge*, Washington, DC, Government Printing Office

Cook, T. (1975), *Vagrant Alcoholics*, London, Routledge & Kegan Paul

Cook, T. (ed.), (1980), *Vagrancy: Some New Perspectives*, London, Academic Press

Cork, R. (1969), *The Forgotten Children: A Study of Children with Alcoholic Parents*, Toronto, Alcoholism and Drug Research Foundation of Ontario

Davies, B. (1975), *The Use of Groups in Social Work Practice*, London, Routledge & Kegan Paul

Davies, D. L. (1962), 'Normal drinking in recovered alcoholics', *Quarterly Journal of Studies on Alcoholism*, vol. 23, pp. 94–104

Davies, J. (1980), 'Alcohol and the Young' in Grant, M. (ed.), *Alcohol Education for Young People in Scotland*, London, Alcohol Education Centre

Davies, J. and Stacey, B. (1972), *Teenagers and Alcohol*, London, HMSO de Lindt, J. and Schmidt, W. (1971), 'Consumption averages and alcoholism prevalence: a brief review of epidemiological investigations', *British Journal of Addictions*, vol. 66, pp. 97–107

Department of Health and Social Services, (1973), *Community Services for Alcoholics*, Department of Health and Social Services, Circular 21/73

Department of Transport, (1980), quoted in Hollerman, S. and Burchall, A. (1981), *The Costs of Alcohol Misuse*, London, DHSS

Dight, S. (1976), *Scottish Drinking Habits*, Edinburgh, HMSO

Douglas, T. (1978), *Groupwork Practice*, London, Tavistock Publications

Edwards, G. (1964), 'The puzzle of AA', *New Society*, May 28

Edwards, G. (1977), 'The Alcohol Dependence Syndrome: The Usefulness of an Idea' in Edwards, G. and Grant, M. *Alcoholism: New Knowledge and Responses*, London, Croom Helm

Edwards, G. and Gross, M. (1976), 'Alcohol dependence: provisional description of a clinical syndrome', *British Medical Journal*, no. 1, pp. 1058–61

Family Discussion Bureau, (1962), *The Marital Relationship as a Focus for Casework*, London, Codicote Press

Glaser, F., Greenberg, S. and Barrett, M. (1978), *A Systems Approach to Alcohol Treatment*, Toronto, Addiction Research Foundation

Glatt, M. (1980), 'The alcoholic and controlled drinking', *British Journal on Alcohol and Alcoholism*, vol. 15, no. 2

Hallett, C. and Stevenson, O. (1980), *Child Abuse: Aspects of Interprofessional Co-operation*, London, George Allen & Unwin

Hartford, M. (1972), *Groups in Social Work*, New York, Columbia University Press

Hawker, A. (1978), *Adolescents and Alcohol*, London, Edsall

Hawker, A. (1979), 'News', *Medical Journal on Alcoholism*, vol. 14, no. 2

Hodgson, R. (1979), 'Much ado about nothing much: alcoholism treatment and the Rand Report', *British Journal of Addictions*, vol. 74, pp. 227–34

Holder, H. and Stratas, N. (1972), 'A systems approach to alcoholism programing', *American Journal of Psychiatry*, July 1972, vol. 129, pp. 32–7

Home Office, (1971), *Habitual Drunken Offenders: Report of the Working Party*, London, HMSO

Home Office, (1972), *Explanatory Memorandum: 1972 Criminal Justice Act*, London, Home Office

Hunt, M. L. (1979), *Communication Process in the Interdisciplinary Team*, M.Sc. thesis, University of Manchester

Jahoda, G. and Crammond, J. (1972), *Children and Alcohol*, London, HMSO

James, J. and Goldman, M. (1971), 'Behaviour trends of wives of alcoholics', *Quarterly Journal of Studies on Alcoholism*, vol. 32, pp. 373–81

Janzen, C. (1978), 'Family treatment for alcoholism: a review', *Social Work*, March 1978

Jarma, C. and Kellett, J. (1979), 'Alcoholism in the general hospital', *British Medical Journal*, no. 2, pp. 469–72

Jellinek, E. M. (1960), *The Disease Concept of Alcoholism*, New Haven, Hillhouse Press

Kendall, R. (1979), 'Alcoholism: a medical or a political problem', *British Medical Journal*, no. 1, pp. 367–71

Kessel, N. and Walton, H. J. (1965), *Alcoholism*, Harmondsworth, Penguin Books

Lee, K., Hardt, F., Moller, L., Haubek, A. and Jensen, E. (1979), 'Alcohol induced brain damage and liver damage in young males', *The Lancet*, vol. 2, no. 8146, pp. 759–61

Lemert, E. (1960), 'The occurrence and sequence of events in the adjustment of families to alcoholism', *Quarterly Journal of Studies on Alcoholism*, vol. 21, pp. 679–97

Levinger, G. (1965), 'Marital cohesiveness and dissolution: an integrative review', *Journal of Marriage and Family*, vol. 27, pp. 19–28

Lewis, M. (1954), 'The initial contact with wives of alcoholics', *Social Casework*, vol. 35, pp. 8–14

Lowry, L. (1970), 'Goal Formulation in Social Work with Groups' in Bernstein, S. (ed.), (1972), *Further Explorations in Group Work*, London, Bookstall Publications

Mattinson, J. and Sinclair, I. (1980), *Mate and Stalemate*, Oxford, Basil Blackwell

Merry, J. (1980), 'Alcoholism in the aged', *British Journal on Alcohol and Alcoholism*, vol. 15, no. 2

Ministry of Health, (1962), *National Health Service: Hospital Treatment of Alcoholism*, HM(62)43

O'Connor, J. (1978), *The Young Drinkers*, London, Tavistock Publications

Orford, J. (1975), 'Alcoholism and marriage: the argument against specialism', *Journal of Studies on Alcohol*, vol. 36, no. 11, pp. 1537–63

Orford, J. (1978), 'Alcohol and the Family' in Grant, M. and Gwinner, P. (eds.), *Alcoholism in Perspective*, London, Croom Helm

Orford, J. and Edwards, G. (1978), *Alcoholism*, Oxford, OUP

Otto, S. and Orford, J. (1978), *Not Quite Like Home: Hostels for Alcoholics and Others*, Chichester, John Wiley & Sons

Perlman, H. (1957), *Social Casework: A Problem-Solving Process*, Chicago, University of Chicago Press

Perlman, H. (1970), 'The Problem Solving Model in Social Casework' in Roberts, R. and Nee, R. *Theories of Social Casework*, Chicago, University of Chicago Press

Petty, M. L. (1975), 'Social work: the profession of choice in the treatment of alcoholism', *Smith College of Social Work Journal*, Fall, 1975

Plant, M. (1977), *Drinking Careers*, London, Tavistock Publications

Plant, M. (1981), Paper presented at conference in Liverpool, April 1981

Polich, J. M., Armor, D. and Braiker, H. (1980), *The Course of Alcoholism: Four Years After Treatment*, Santa Monica, California, The Rand Corporation

Pollak, B. (1970), 'The role of the general practitioner in support of an alcoholic rehabilitation hostel', *British Journal of Addictions*, vol. 65, pp. 19–24

Priestley, P., McGuire, J., Flegg, D., Hemsley, V. and Welham, D. (1978), *Social Skills and Personal Problem Solving*, London, Tavistock Publications

Rapoport, L. (1965), 'The State of Crisis: Some Theoretical Considerations' in Parad, H. (ed.), *Crisis Intervention: Selected Readings*, New York, Family Service Association of America

Rapoport, L. (1970), 'Crisis Intervention as a Mode of Brief Treatment' in Roberts, R. and Nee, R. *Theories of Social Casework*, Chicago, University of Chicago Press

Ritson, E. B. (1977), 'Alcoholism and Suicide' in Edwards, G. and Grant, M. (eds.), *Alcoholism: New Knowledge and Responses*, London, Croom Helm

Ritson, E. B. (1981), *Personal Communication*

Roberts, R. and Northen, H. (eds.), (1976), *Theories of Social Work with Groups*, New York, Columbia University Press

Robinson, D. (1976), *From Drinking to Alcoholism*, Chichester, John Wiley & Sons

Robinson, D. (1979), *Talking Out of Alcoholism: The self-help process of AA*, London, Croom Helm

Royal College of Psychiatrists, (1979), *Alcohol and Alcoholism*, London, Tavistock Publications

Rueveni, U. (1979), *Networking Families in Crisis*, London, Human Sciences Press

Schmidt, W. (1977), 'Cirrhosis and Alcohol Consumption', in Edwards, G. and Grant, M. (eds.), *Alcoholism: New Knowledge and Responses*, London, Croom Helm

Sclare, A. B. (1979), 'Alcoholism in doctors', *British Journal of Alcohol and Alcoholism*, vol. 14, no. 4, pp. 181–96

Sclare, A. B. (1980), 'The Foetal Alcohol Syndrome' in Camberwell Council on Alcoholism, *Women and Alcohol*, London, Tavistock Publications

Semple, B. and Yarrow, A. (1974), 'Health education, alcohol and alcoholism in Scotland', *Health Bulletin*, vol. 32, no. 1

Shaw, S. (1980), 'The Causes of Increasing Drinking Problems in Women' in Camberwell Council on Alcoholism, *Women and Alcohol*, London, Tavistock Publications

Shaw, S., Cartwright, A., Spratley, T. and Harwin, J. (1978), *Responding to Drinking Problems*, London, Croom Helm

Skynner, R. (1976), *One Flesh, Separate Persons*, London, Constable

Sobell, M. and Sobell, L. (1976), 'Second year treatment outcome of alcoholics treated by individualised behaviour therapy' *Behaviour Research and Therapy*, vol. 14, pp. 195–215

Social Work Services Group, (1976), *Community Services for Alcoholics*, Edinburgh, Social Work Services Group, Circular SW4/1976

Social Work Services Group, (1980), *Social Work Case Statistics 1979*, Statistical Bulletin, Edinburgh, Social Work Services Group

Stacey, B. and Davies, J. (1970), 'Drinking behaviour in childhood and adolescence: an evaluative review', *British Journal of Addictions*, vol. 65, pp. 203–12

Steinglass, P. (1976), 'Experimenting with family treatment approaches to alcoholism, 1950–1975, a review', *Family Process*, vol. 15, pp. 97–123

Steiner, C. (1971), *Games Alcoholics Play*, New York, Grove Press

Strathclyde Social Work Committee, (1978), *Addiction, Collusion or Cover Up?* Report of an Officer/Member Group, Strathclyde Regional Council

Tsuang, M. and Vandermey, R. (1980), *Genes and the Mind*, Oxford, OUP

Walrond-Skinner, S. (1976), *Family Therapy: The Treatment of Natural Systems*, London, Routledge & Kegan Paul

Whalen, T. (1953), 'Wives of alcoholics: four types observed in a family service agency', *Quarterly Journal of Studies on Alcohol*, vol. 14, pp. 632–41

Wilkins, R. (1974), *The Hidden Alcoholic in General Practice*, London, Elek (Scientific Books)

Wilson, C. and Orford, J. (1978), 'Children of alcoholics: report of a preliminary study and comments on the literature', *Journal of Studies on Alcohol*, vol. 39, no. 1, pp. 121–42

World Health Organisation Expert Committee on Mental Health, (1952), *Alcohol Sub-Committee Second Report*, WHO Technical Report Series, no. 48

Zimberg, S. (1978), 'Psychosocial Treatment of Elderly Alcoholics' in Zimberg, S. Wallace, J. and Blume, S. (eds.), *Practical Approaches to Alcoholism Psychotherapy*, New York, Plenum Press

Index